THE GOLOVLYOVS

A Critical Companion

T0325529

SALTYKOV-SHCHEDRIN'S

THE GOLOVLYOVS

A Critical Companion

Edited by I. P. Foote

Northwestern University Press

The American Association of Teachers of

Slavic and East European Languages

Northwestern University Press

Evanston, Illinois 60208-4210

Copyright © 1997 by

Northwestern University Press

All rights reserved

Printed in the United States of America

ISBN 0-8101-1311-2

Library of Congress Cataloging-in-Publication Data

Saltykov-Shchedrin's The Golovlyovs : a critical companion / edited by

I. P. Foote.

p.   cm. — (Northwestern/AATSEEL critical companions to

Russian literature)

Includes bibliographical references.

ISBN 0-8101-1311-2 (alk. paper)

1. Saltykov, Mikhail Evgrafovich, 1826–1889. Gospoda Golovlevy.

I. Foote, I. P. (Irwin Paul)   II. Series.

PG3361.S3G6385   1997

891.73 3—dc21   97-31164

                                                                                  CIP

The paper used in this publication meets

the minimum requirements of the

American National Standard for Information

Sciences – Permanence of Paper for Printed

Library Materials, ANSI z39.48-1984.

Contents

Acknowledgments

Much of the material in this volume has been previously published. Grateful acknowledgment is made to authors, journals, and publishers to reprint copyrighted material.

A. M. Skabichevskii, "Blagonamerennye rechi g. Shchedrina," *Sankt-Peterburgskie vedomosti*, no. 307 (1875); Denisiuk, *Kriticheskaia literatura o proizvedeniiakh M. E. Saltykova-Shchedrina* (Moscow: Izdanie A. S. Panafidinoi, 1905), 2:299–301.

V. V. Markov, "'Vymorochnyi' N. Shchedrina," *Sankt-Peterburgskie vedomosti*, no. 265 (1876); Denisiuk, *Kriticheskaia literatura* 3:113–15.

M. [A.] Protopopov, "Kharakteristiki sovremennykh deiatelei, 1. M. E. Saltykov-Shchedrin," *Delo*, no. 4 (1883): 328–38.

K. Golovin, from *Russkii roman i russkoe obshchestvo* (St. Petersburg, 1897; Denisiuk, *Kriticheskaia literatura* 5:270–72).

A. I. Vvedenskii, from *Literaturnye kharakteristiki* (St. Petersburg, 1903; Denisiuk, *Kriticheskaia literatura* 3:287–90).

A. S. Bushmin, from *Satira Saltykova-Shchedrina* (Moscow-Leningrad: Akademiia nauk, 1959), 187–91.

K. N. Grigor'ian, *Roman M. E. Saltykova-Shchedrina "Gospoda Golovlyovy"* (Moscow-Leningrad: Nauka, 1962), 60–64.

V. V. Prozorov, from *Saltykov-Shchedrin. Kniga dlia uchitelia* (Moscow: "Prosveshchenie," 1988). Reprinted by permission.

Nikander Strelsky, from *Saltykov and the Russian Squire* (New York: Columbia University Press, 1940). Copyright © 1940 by Columbia University Press. Reprinted by permission of the publisher.

V. S. Pritchett, "The Hypocrite," in Pritchett's *The Living Novel* (London: Chatto and Windus, 1946). Copyright © 1946 by V. S. Pritchett. Reprinted by permission of The Peters Fraser and Dunlop Group Limited on behalf of the author.

I. P. Foote, extract from "M. E. Saltykov-Shchedrin: *The Golovlyov*

Family," in *Forum for Modern Language Studies* (January 1968). Reprinted by permission of the publisher.

Milton Ehre, "A Classic of Russian Realism: Form and Meaning in *The Golovlyovs,*" in *Studies in the Novel*, vol. 9 (Spring 1977): 3–16. Copyright © 1977 by the University of North Texas. Reprinted by permission of the publisher.

Karl D. Kramer, "Satiric Form in Saltykov's *Gospoda Golovlevy,*" *Slavic and East European Journal* 14 (1970): 453–64. Reprinted by permission of the publisher.

⸺

Thanks are also due to Alison Cowe for her helpful comments and suggestions.

A Note on Translation and Transliteration

The transliteration system used is that of the Library of Congress, except in the case of the name Golovlyov. The spelling "Golovlyov" has been preferred, because it is the form most commonly found in modern translations and for the non-Russian reader indicates most clearly how it is pronounced (the stress is on the final syllable); in bibliographical references, however, the Library of Congress form (Golovlëv) is used. The transliteration in English-language articles reprinted from other sources has been modified for consistency. All translations from the Russian are my own. – ED.

I ❄ INTRODUCTION

Saltykov and *The Golovlyovs*

I. P. FOOTE

M. E. Saltykov (pen name "Shchedrin," thus commonly known as "Saltykov-Shchedrin") is less well known to the general reading public than other leading Russian writers of his time – Turgenev, Tolstoy, Dostoevsky, Goncharov, for example – but during a literary career that spanned four decades (from the 1840s to the 1880s), and particularly from the 1860s on, he was a dominant figure on the Russian literary scene. He was a prolific writer, his works were widely read, and he had a formidable reputation as co-editor and then chief editor of the leading radical journal *Otechestvennye zapiski* (*Notes of the Fatherland*; henceforward, *NF*). That he is little known today is simply explained: he was not primarily a novelist but, in the literal and best sense, a journalist, whose main concern was to describe and reflect on the events and movements in Russian society of his day. His works as a whole constitute a chronicle, usually sharply satirical, of his times, and to his contemporaries he offered, as he still offers to the historically initiated, a unique analysis of Russian society in a period of crisis caused by social change, reform and counter-reform, and conflict between the government and the growing forces of political opposition. Gorky did not overrate Saltykov when he remarked that it was impossible to understand the history of Russia in the second half of the nineteenth century without a knowledge of Saltykov's works. If the greater part of Saltykov's writings are, because of their local and contemporary interest, out of reach to the modern reader (and to the foreign reader in any case because of lack of translations), there are two or three that are of permanent interest and easy access: one of these is his novel *Gospoda Golovlyovy* (*The Golovlyovs*).[1]

For his role as analyst and commentator on his society Saltykov was extremely well qualified. He was born in 1826, the son of a well-to-do landowning family in the province of Tver'. Though his family was characterized by many of the uncouth features of the Golovlyovs (their affinities will be mentioned below), Saltykov was educated in the best institutions of the day – the Moscow Pension for the Nobility and the Alexander Lycée in St Petersburg. On graduating in 1844 he entered the civil service as an official of the War Ministry in St. Petersburg, and there moved in literary and intellectual circles where he was influenced by the then fashionable French Utopian socialist ideas. He made his literary debut in 1847–48 with a couple of stories, one of which was deemed "subversive" and caused his exile in 1848 to Viatka. There he spent seven years in the provincial administration, which furnished him with valuable firsthand experience of provincial life, the peasants and their problems, and the workings of the bureaucracy. He returned to St. Petersburg in 1856, newly married to Elizaveta Boltina, daughter of a Viatka senior official, and continued his service career, first in the capital, then as vice-governor in the provinces of Riazan' (1858–60) and Tver' (1860–62). He simultaneously engaged in writing (from 1856 on) and gained fame with his *Gubernskie ocherki* (*Provincial sketches* [1856–57]), which were based on his experiences in Viatka. In 1862 he left the civil service and joined the editorial staff of the radical journal *Sovremennik* (*The contemporary*), to which he was a notable contributor of sketches on contemporary life, reviews, and articles in the polemical battle then raging between journals of different political tendencies. For reasons financial and ideological he returned to government service in 1864 and was director of finance in the provinces of Penza (1865–66), Tula (1866–67), and Riazan' (1867–68). Under official pressure he retired from the service in 1868 as an official of the fourth grade (equivalent to the military rank of major general) and devoted himself thereafter to literary work, becoming first joint editor (with Nekrasov and Eliseev) and then, from 1878 on, chief editor of *NF*, which was the spiritual successor of the now suppressed *Contemporary*. For sixteen years until *NF*'s suppression (1884) Saltykov was a dominant force on the journal and a regular contributor to its monthly issues. After 1884 he continued to write, publishing in other journals, until his death in 1889. As this brief sketch of his life shows, Saltykov was from practical experience thoroughly acquainted with Russian life in all its main aspects and at all levels of society – in Turgenev's view, he "knew Russia better than any living man": his assessment of his country's condition was as severe as his knowledge of it was broad.

Saltykov's standard literary product was the monthly sketch or essay of "journal" length (twenty to thirty pages) on a particular theme of the day. As a rule, a theme would be elaborated in a succession of sketches published over a period of months (in some cases, longer) and, when finally completed, the whole "cycle" would appear in book form under a common title, – for example, *Provincial Sketches, Satires in Prose, Letters on the Provinces, Trivia of Life*. The items in these cycles were of two main types: the discursive essay and the narrative sketch; sometimes the two modes of exposition were used in the same piece. It was in one of these cycles that *The Golovlyovs* had its origin.

In 1872 Saltykov began publishing in *NF* a series of sketches entitled *Blagonamerennye rechi* (*Well-Intentioned Speeches*), in which his purpose was to expose the hollowness of certain principles claimed by the "establishment" and its publicists as the bases on which Russian society rested – the principles of state, family, and property. In his sketches Saltykov set out to show that those who proclaimed these principles in words (the "well-intentioned speeches" of the title)[2] systematically flouted them in their deeds. In 1874–75 the question of the family was broached in a number of sketches in the cycle: in "Stolp" (The pillar, January 1874) Derunov, a "pillar of society," has an illicit relationship with his daughter-in-law; in "Eshchë perepiska" (A further correspondence, October 1874) the Prokaznins, mother and son, exchange cynical letters about their immoral affairs; in "Otets i syn" (Father and son, March 1875) General Utrobin's son connives with a local entrepreneur to dispossess his father of his estate; and in "Nepochtitel'nyi Koronat" (Disrespectful Koronat, November 1875) the "principled" Cousin

Mashen'ka is at odds with her idealistic son who wishes to decide his own course in life. In all cases, family relations are bad. "Family Court," which was to become the first chapter of *The Golovlyovs*,[3] was published as part of the cycle in October 1875 and its message was the same. In it we are presented with the Golovlyov family (to which passing reference is made also in "Disrespectful Koronat") and see the harsh judgment passed on the wayward Stepan Golovlyov by his imperious mother, Arina Petrovna. It set the tone for the succeeding sketches in the Golovlyov "chronicle": the "family," declared as a sacred foundation of society, is exposed as a corrupt institution whose dominant characteristics are malice, greed, and treachery.

The next three sketches, appearing still under the rubric of *Well-Intentioned Speeches*, were published in December 1875 ("Kith and Kin"), March 1876 ("Family Scores"), and May 1876 ("Before Es-cheatment," called in Saltykov's correspondence before publication "Escheated," later revised and retitled "The Niece"). Saltykov had been encouraged to continue the Golovlyov theme by the positive reaction to the first sketches (Turgenev, whose opinion Saltykov particularly respected, gave them high praise)[4] and by May 1876 he was expressing regret that he had included them in *Well-Intentioned Speeches* and had not published them separately as *Episodes from the History of a Family*.[5] The development of Porfirii ("Judas") Golovlyov, who since "Kith and Kin" had emerged as the dominat-ing figure of the "chronicle," had now been carried so far and aroused such interest that Saltykov felt obliged to write a further chapter (as it turned out to be, further chapters) to show his "end." This led, first, to "Escheated" (August 1876) and then to the chapter "Family Joys" (December 1876, the title later expanded to "Illicit Family Joys"), which elaborated on a passing reference in "Esche-ated" (the journal version, that is) to Porfirii's fathering a bastard son by his housekeeper, Evpraksiia. In a footnote to "Family Joys" Saltykov announced that "one more story" would conclude the novel. A first attempt to finish it (the uncompleted "U pristani" ("Haven Home")[6] was abandoned – probably in 1877 – and the work was finally completed only in 1880 with "The Resolution"

(May 1880, later retitled "The Reckoning"). In July 1880 the novel was issued in a separate edition; a second, slightly revised edition was published in 1883.

The journal text was revised for the separate edition. Apart from some trimming and minor adjustments to achieve consistency, no significant changes were made in the first four chapters. Substantial revision was necessary for "Illicit Family Joys" and "Escheated," as Saltykov had indicated in his note to the former when published in *NF*.[7] To match the sequence of events, the order of these chapters was reversed, with "Illicit Family Joys" preceding "Escheated." Numerous cuts were made from "Escheated" (more than a fifth of the journal text): some of these were of passages transferred to "Illicit Family Joys" (for example, the Porfirii-Ulita interview to settle the fate of Evpraksiia's baby); others were made, evidently, to avoid excessive length. Brevity was also the probable reason for deleting a few passages from "Illicit Family Joys," though in one or two cases there may have been other considerations.[8] "The Reckoning," apart from the new title,[9] repeated the journal text with only a few minor changes.

The Golovlyovs is a story of degeneration and decline. Three generations of the family are presented in the novel: the matriarch Arina Petrovna and her feeble husband Vladimir Mikhailovich; their sons Stepan, Pavel, and Porfirii; and their grandchildren Petia and Volodia (sons of Porfirii) and Annin'ka and Liubin'ka (the twin offspring of a deceased daughter, Annushka, who had fallen from favor by making a run-away marriage). By the end of the novel all of them – except Annin'ka, who is mortally ill – are dead: it is, as one critic described it, "one long obituary."

Saltykov, as was said, began the Golovlyov sketches as part of *Well-Intentioned Speeches*, in which he set out to expose the sham of society's principles of state, family, and property. "I wrote *The Golovlyovs* as an attack on the family principle," he declared in a letter of 1881[10] – and his attack could hardly have been more damning. The family he depicts is one destitute of all family feeling. Among the Golovlyovs there is no love, no generosity of spirit, no common interest. The only operative family principle is that of children's obedience to their parents. Children who obey may receive meager favors, those who do not are cut off. The family "affections" are malice, envy, and hatred – well exemplified in the names they apply to one another: "blackguard," "swine," "bloodsucker" (Arina Petrovna of her sons); "blackguard," "scoundrel" (Porfirii of his son Petia); "murdering Judas" (Petia of his father); and so on. The irony is that the "family" is most loudly proclaimed by the two family tyrants, Arina Petrovna and Porfirii, who between them cause the ruin and destruction of their offspring and siblings: Arina Petrovna accumulates wealth "for the family," which she oppresses and neglects; Porfirii, to the refrain of "kith and kin," dispossesses his mother and brothers and condemns his sons to disgrace and suicide.

The gentry family was a well-established theme in Russian literature from the 1830s on. Family relations had figured prominently in warm, reminiscent accounts of childhood by S. T. Aksakov, Tolstoy, Goncharov; "gentry nests" and their cultivated occupants had been described in a succession of stories and novels by Turgenev; *War and Peace*, Tolstoy's great family epic, had appeared in the 1860s. The general picture of home life among the gentry had been wholesome and sympathetic. By the 1870s, however, the perspective had changed. Tolstoy's *Anna Karenina* (1875–77) presented, in contrast to *War and Peace*, the instability of family life in the Karenins (only dubiously balanced by the wholesome Levins); Dostoevsky, in *The Brothers Karamazov* (1879–80), portrayed the moral dissolution of the family (a decade earlier, in *Crime and Punishment*, even the "outsider" Raskolnikov had normal family affections). *The Golovlyovs*, written at the same time, offers the starkest example of this new "family" novel.

In choosing a family of provincial landowners to exemplify his thesis on the family principle, Saltykov was entering a broader field of social criticism. While presenting his negative picture of the Golovlyovs as a *family*, he was at the same time passing judgment on the class to which they (and he) belonged. He not only showed, in common with his contemporaries, the disintegration of the family, but he also indicated the degenerate state of the gentry class. The Golovlyovs – uncouth, morally corrupt, lacking vitality and social purpose – offer a sharp contrast to the humane and civilized society presented in earlier gentry novels (although Gogol had, in *Dead Souls*, given a similar obverse view with his grotesque gallery of landowners, and Goncharov's stagnant Oblomovka, with less benign occupants, might have been another Golovlyovo). Golovlyovo, if not typical of all gentry households, was still a warning symbol of what the decline of the class could lead to. And it was not a symbol conjured up in the author's imagination, for Saltykov, in depicting the Golovlyovs, drew on his own experience and roughly portrayed in the principal characters members of his own family.

Relations in the Saltykov family, between parents and sons and between the sons themselves, were mostly hostile, as is clear from the evidence of contemporaries and the family correspondence (in which epithets such as "villain" and "scoundrel" are – in true Golovlyov fashion – freely bestowed). N. A. Belogolovyi, Saltykov's friend and doctor, described the family as "savage and ill-tempered" and relations between its members as "marked by an animal cruelty, devoid of any warm familial aspects."[11] Ol'ga Mikhailovna, Saltykov's mother, was closely portrayed in Arina Petrovna,[12] the life and death of his brother Nikolai are reflected in the story of Stepan Golovlyov,[13] features of his brother Sergei are found in Pavel, and in Porfirii the author paid off his scores with his detested eldest brother Dmitrii.[14] The family was rent by disputes, chiefly over property: a division of family estates in 1859, disadvantageous to Saltykov, had soured his relations with Dmitrii; after the death of Sergei in 1872 a long and bitter quarrel arose between them over Dmitrii's machinations to deprive Saltykov of his full share of the inheritance. In a letter to Unkovskii, Saltykov bluntly stated the Dmitrii-Pofirii connection: "It was him I depicted in the character of Judas."[15] In view of the novel's close associations with his own family, note that it was only after the death (in 1874) of Ol'ga Mikhailovna that Saltykov, who held her always in fearful regard, ventured on his revelation of the family mores. It should of course be emphasized that *The*

Golovlyovs, like certain other works by Saltykov,[16] though depicting characters inspired by his family, does not recount family history (though "Family Court" comes close); Belogolovyi records Saltykov's statement on *The Golovlyovs* that "he took from reality only the characters, but in developing the theme of the story and the fate of the dramatis personae gave much play to invention."[17]

The novel covers a period of about twenty years, from around 1856 to 1877/8, with some reference back (in Arina Petrovna's reminiscences) to the 1820s. The Golovlyovs who are modeled most closely on Saltykov's family (i.e. the old Golovlyovs and the three sons) are of an age that roughly accords with their real-life prototypes. "Family Court" is set shortly after the Crimean War (which ended in 1855), "Kith and Kin" is "ten years on," and the events of the succeeding chapters take place in the 1870s. Saltykov does not follow an exact chronology, and although there are one or two inconsistencies (a reference to the 1870 siege of Paris in "Kith and Kin" (1866/7) and Porfirii's unlikely – given his age – "thirty years" spent as an official), they are of little significance. There is reference here and there to events in Russia of the time, which saw the major reforms initiated by Alexander II: the emancipation of the serfs in 1861 (the event, anticipated and actual, referred to in "Kith and Kin" and some of its consequences in "Escheated"), the introduction of new court procedures and the rise of professional advocates in 1864 (lawyers occur in "Kith and Kin," "Family Scores," and "The Reckoning"), and the establishment of new local government institutions (*zemstvos*) also in 1864 (referred to in "The Reckoning"). The most important of these reforms – the emancipation – had serious economic consequences for many landowners but seems to have had no adverse effect on the Golovlyovs – the estate continues to prosper and Porfirii is (in "The Niece") "the biggest landowner in the whole district." Only the ailing Arina Petrovna is shaken by it, but this is no more than the psychological shock at seeing her familiar world being turned upside down.

The focus of the novel is strictly on the members of the Golovlyov family. The scene of action is restricted, similarly, to

Golovlyovo and the lesser family estates of Dubrovino (property of Pavel) and Pogorelka (property of Annin'ka and Liubin'ka). Non-family characters, with the exception of Porfirii's housekeeper and mistress Evpraksiia, are incidental (domestics, peasants, the local clergy and doctor). Only in the account of the theatrical career of the nieces (in "The Niece" and "The Reckoning"), which anyway is retrospective, is there any shift of location or reference to other social milieux. This concentration of interest serves to emphasize that the degeneration of the Golovlyovs is an internal process and not the result of any external influences or circumstances. Golovlyovo is the seat and source of the family malaise, and it stands as a symbol of the family's malign destiny: Stepan returns to it as to a "coffin," Annin'ka sees it as "death itself, malign, empty-hearted . . . , ever watchful for some fresh victim."

The process of family degeneration is already evident in the older generation. Vladimir Mikhailovich, the father, is a frivolous, tippling roué, good for nothing, a "stringless balalaika" in Arina Petrovna's phrase. Arina Petrovna herself, the one character in the novel who has vigour and practical ability, is not, of course, of Golovlyov stock. She has married into the family and, though it is not stated, it might be supposed that she, like Saltykov's mother, had her origins in the merchant class, which was certainly not lacking in the entrepreneurial vitality that characterizes her. Although Arina Petrovna increases the Golovlyov property, her despotic and dismissive treatment of her children accelerates, if anything, the family's moral decline. We see the Golovlyov sons in their later years. In "Family Court" there is passing reference to them as boys, with characteristics that presage their future development: Stepan, talented but irresponsible; Pavel, taciturn and sullen; Porfirii, enigmatic and treacherous. Stepan fritters away his substance and his life. Pavel and Porfirii follow the common course of gentry sons and serve in the army (Pavel) and civil service (Porfirii), but they make no mark; these years spent outside Golovlyovo are passed over by Saltykov and we see these characters only on their home ground after they have retired. They have made nothing of their lives because their personalities were suppressed or distorted by the family regime of Go-lovlyovo. The third generation (Volodia, Petia, Annin'ka, and Liubin'ka) shows a further – and final – stage in the family decline: Volodia and Liubin'ka end their lives by suicide; Petia dies in a convict convoy en route to Siberia; Annin'ka, broken by her disso-lute life as an actress, returns to Golovlyovo to die. At the end of the novel the process of degeneration is complete and the line extinct.

None of the Golovlyovs has any higher ideals or aspirations, none is capable of any useful activity. Their chief lack is of any *moral substance* that might provide them with direction and purpose in life. The inner "emptiness," which is characteristic of them all, finds its fullest expression in Porfirii. The Russian word *pustoi* (empty) ap-pears in three recurring thematic words that sum up his personality: *pustoslovie* (empty talk),[18] *pustomyslie* (empty thought), and *pustou-trobie* (empty inward parts, i.e., spiritually hollow; the second ele-ment in the compound is *utroba*, meaning womb or belly). The first two are merely manifestations of the last, which indicates precisely the lack of that inner substance which is the source of moral strength and human dignity. The Golovlyov brothers all die wretchedly, as-sisted to the grave by drink. The younger generation, unequipped for life, flounder and sink. Annin'ka alone has the spirit, if not the strength, to struggle against her fate, but her efforts are misdirected and she, too, falls victim to Golovlyovo.

Debased as they are, the Golovlyovs evoke, by their very wretch-edness, some sort of sympathy in the reader. The response is natural enough in the case of Stepan, Pavel, and the grandchildren, who fall victim to the family tyrants, but surprisingly even the tyrants in the end stir a measure of pity as we see them realizing too late the destructive futility of their lives. The principal Golovlyovs are all isolated souls, cut off from human contact in the family or outside it. Confined within their own personalities as they are within the walls of their manor houses, lacking moral sense or purpose, they perform a ritual of living that has form (if that), but no substance. It may be a ritual of activity (Arina Petrovna and Porfirii) or of inactivity (Stepan and Pavel), but it amounts to the same thing – a life devoid of meaning. In the end, clearly or dimly, they realize this and despair. Faced with the hopeless reality of their lives, the sons, as also Annin'ka in the end, take to drink in order to blot it out. There is an element of tragedy in the death throes of these stricken souls, which Saltykov describes in a succession of memorably harrowing scenes.

In the first four chapters of *The Golovlyovs* Saltykov had amply fulfilled his intention to expose the sham of the "family principle" and had also settled his account with his brother Dmitrii. It was his purpose at this point to write a final chapter to round off the se-quence of Golovlyov sketches. In the event, he wrote three more chapters, since he had in Porfirii created a major character of serious psychological interest who, he felt (and was encouraged by others to feel), required further development. Porfirii had emerged in "Kith and Kin" as the co-principal protagonist (with Arina Petrovna); thereafter he becomes the central focus of the novel. Though the family theme remains relevant in the following chapters, they are primarily concerned with the exposition and analysis of Porfirii's character. The novel that had begun as an investigation of a social institution becomes a psychological novel focusing on an individual.

After the second chapter, attention is centered on three of the surviving Golovlyovs, one from each generation: Arina Petrovna, Porfirii, and Annin'ka. It is these characters whom Saltykov treats most fully. Stepan and Pavel, skillfully portrayed in "Family Court" and "Kith and Kin," are static characters and undergo no develop-ment. Arina Petrovna, Porfirii, and Annin'ka play out longer roles, and the perspective on each is changed as the novel progresses.

Arina Petrovna, the dominant figure in "Family Scores," begins her decline in "Kith and Kin"; it continues in "Family Scores," and ends with her death in "The Niece." She is "resurrected" in the retrospective "Illicit Family Joys" and makes a fleeting appearance in Porfirii's fantasies in "Escheated." In the course of these chapters the initial view of her as the inflexible, hard-hearted family despot is considerably modified. She is a hard woman, but she has had a hard life and had to make her way in a hard world. She has driven herself – senselessly – to increase the family property and to amass provisions from which her stringent economy allows no one to benefit; by her harsh domestic rule she has deformed her children, whom she regards as unworthy claimants to the fruits of her toil, and made a mockery of the "family principle" she claims to uphold. Yet there is a rough humanity about her, which gradually is revealed. She already shows a twinge of feeling in "Family Court" when she warns Porfirii against beggaring Stepan, and in subsequent chapters – admittedly as her powers decline – we see her accepting her granddaughters' strivings for a "better" life outside Golovlyovo, being gruffly amiable with her grandchildren, feeling outrage at Porfirii's treatment of Petia (for which she curses him), and engaging with relish in the business of Evpraksiia's pregnancy. A certain kind of human warmth is also suggested – throughout – by her robust, homely speech and occasional rough humor. The poignant description of her physical decline and transformation from all-powerful despot to helpless dependent also tends to reconcile her to the reader, as does the fact that at the end of her life she realizes, albeit dimly, that her endeavors have been futile and that life can be lived in ways other than the one she followed.

Annin'ka's development is entirely within the novel; we follow her progress from artless girl in "Kith and Kin" to demoralized provincial actress in "The Niece" and "The Reckoning," the two chapters in which she plays a principal part. Annin'ka is the nearest the novel offers to a positive character, and her role is an important one. She has spirit, even some strength of character; she rejects Golovlyovo and follows her naive aspirations for a better life outside it. Without any serious education or ability and lacking, critically, any solid moral foundation (the result of her Golovlyovo upbringing), she comes to grief in the world she enters. Even there she shows some strength; she does not fall readily (as her sister does) to the sordid blandishments of the Liul'kins and Kukishevs, and, in the painfully lucid intervals when she returns to Golovlyovo, she feels revulsion for the way of life to which she has succumbed. There is a positive element even in her attempted self-delusion of "serving Art" in her career as an actress: she feels at least the *need* to delude herself. Her major positive feature, however, is that she has the clarity of vision to recognize Golovlyovo as the source of her corruption and the strength to resist and finally denounce Porfirii. It is she who breaks him, sowing the seeds of his downfall by her subversion of Evpraksiia in "The Niece" and completing it by the judgment she pronounces in "The Reckoning." It is she, too, who in the final scene discerns the truth of his repentance and, by her compassionate embrace, symbolically returns him to the human fold.

Arina Petrovna and Annin'ka, for all their importance, are, however, only adjuncts to the central character, Porfirii. In many respects Porfirii *is* the novel, and one can understand, if not accept, the decision of the editors of the 1957 Moscow translation to entitle it *Judas Golovlyov*. In Porfirii, Saltykov created a unique figure who rightly occupies a place among the "great characters" of Russian literature. Few literary works have had such an odious and repellent main character. He is mean, cunning, treacherous, and, above all, a man of monumental pettiness and breathtaking hypocrisy. Although Saltykov's portrayal of him is uninhibitedly tendentious, bordering at times on caricature, still the character has a chilling credibility and offers a subject for serious social and psychological analysis.

Porfirii's essential characteristics are established by his first appearance in "Family Court." Already as a child he has been dubbed "Judas," "Bloodsucker," and "Candid Lad,"[19] and in this first chapter we see evidence of his hypocrisy (his pious gestures and expressions of obedience to Arina Petrovna) and his treachery (dissuading his mother from conceding further property to Stepan). Thereafter his character burgeons; in successive chapters we see him tormenting, exploiting, and ruining the other members of his family. He mocks the dying Pavel with his cynical solicitations, exploits and dispossesses his mother, makes unseemly advances to his niece Annin'ka, causes the ruin and death of his two sons, embitters Evpraksiia by taking from her the baby he has fathered, and dispatches the same infant to likely death in a foundlings' home.[20] Along the way he torments neighbours, peasants, and servants with his impositions, pettifogging litigation, and endless moralizing cant.

What is truly outrageous about Porfirii is not so much his deeds, which are bad enough, as his continual proclamations of being a good family man, an upholder of the "family principle," declaring his every action to be in accord with "right," "the law," or "the will of God." While plotting and performing his dark deeds, he presents himself as a model of Christian piety, forever praying, crossing himself, citing Scripture, and looking to icons. He is rightly renowned as a classic hypocrite. Early in the novel (in "Family Scores") Saltykov included a lengthy digression on the nature of Porfirii's hypocrisy. He was prompted to do so because reviews of the preceding chapters had referred to Porfirii as "a Russian Tartuffe."[21] In this digression, Saltykov sets out the differences between the Russian hypocrite and his French counterpart represented by Tartuffe and the hypocrites of modern French bourgeois society, which Saltykov observed firsthand when he was in France for health reasons in 1875–76. He differentiates the two on the grounds that in France hypocrisy is a prop to society, since it recognizes that there are standards which must, at least outwardly, be maintained, whereas in Russia such hypocrisy cannot exist because Russia has *no* social standards to maintain: the Russian hypocrite is therefore a mere "scoundrel, liar, and prattler (*pustoslov*)." This statement is in keeping with the theme of *Well-Intentioned Speeches* (that the proclaimed "bases" of Russian society do not in fact exist), and, since Saltykov was still writing about the Golovlyovs within the rubric of this cycle, he found it opportune to make this distinction between the Russian and French varieties of the hypocrite. The essential difference he points to is that between two societies (one with "bases" and one without); the different types of hypocrite are merely their products. No doubt the reviewers who called Porfirii a "Russian Tartuffe" were using the name as a byword for "hypocrite" rather than with strict reference to the character in Molière's play. But if a comparison is drawn between the two literary hypocrites, a significant distinction emerges – while for Molière's character hypocrisy is a conscious tactical device (Tartuffe is a confidence trickster who pretends piety to win the daughter and wealth of the gullible Orgon), for Porfirii it is an inherent attribute of his deformed nature.

Porfirii's dominating – and most nauseating – feature is his addiction to empty talk (*pustoslovie*). He talks incessantly in an unending flow of banalities: lecturing, moralizing, and discoursing on the weather, the size of melons, and any other trivial topic that occurs to him. His tone at times is pious, at times jocular; sometimes in the mesh of words there is a hidden purpose as Porfirii "casts a snare" or "weaves a web" to trap some victim ("every word you say means ten different things," his son Petia tells him). The language he uses is full of homely words and forms of the kind used in speaking to familiars or children – another deception, since this affable manner of speech is only a screen to the speaker's sinister intentions.

This flow of "verbal pus" is, for Porfirii, a means of exerting his tyranny over others – by words he torments and bores them into submission (a peasant remarks that "with his talk he can rot a man's soul"). It also has the function of providing a barrier for him against life's circumstances and making him secure against all eventualities. In "Family Scores" Saltykov writes:

> Judas is always prepared for *anything* in advance. He knows . . . that *nothing* can make him depart from that web of empty, putrid aphorisms with which he has enveloped himself from head to toe. For him there exists neither sorrow nor joy, neither hatred nor love. The whole world in his eyes is a tomb, fit only to serve as a pretext for his endless empty talk.

Porfirii has no inner being, no normal human impulses. His life is based on the performance of ritual: his meaningless talk is a ritual, and there are the set-piece rituals he performs – the sessions of prayer, the gestures of piety, the routine leave-taking of family members (Arina Petrovna, Petia, Annin'ka, the baby Volodka – all of whom he has grievously injured), his slow eating (a deliberate irritant to his guests), and so on. Ritual is evident, too, in his activities as owner of the Golovlyovo estate: his "management" is concerned only with formalities – profitless litigation, senseless record keeping, and idle calculations that have no relevance to reality.[22]

Porfirii's hypocrisy, his empty verbiage, his empty rituals are all outward forms that conceal the moral vacuum within him. Form over substance is the key to his character. He has no vision, no grand scheme, no final purpose. He would seem to be motivated by greed – for property and for power – but when he attains these, they bring him no benefit other than the opportunity to regulate things (and people) according to his own pettifogging systems. His nature is trivial, rather than evil, and his villainies are performed without passion, as a matter of compulsive routine: he routinely seizes on any situation that allows him to play a dirty trick and routinely justifies it with one of his ever ready aphorisms. Porfirii's "successes" are not achieved by overcoming opposition, for he preys only on the weak and vulnerable: he exploits Arina Petrovna when her powers have declined, ensures that no further property goes to the already down-and-out Stepan, torments Pavel as he lies dying, turns his sons away when they are helpless; in the same way, he exploits his needy peasant neighbors with his loans and exactions (to quote from "Escheated": "It is round these helpless souls, these destitute poor that Judas spins his endless web"). Dire though the consequences of Porfirii's actions may be for others, for him their main significance seems to be as exercises for his ingenuity and humbug. Porfirii's exploits, for the reader, have even a kind of grim entertainment value as he waits to see what outrage he will next perform and with what moralizing platitudes he will manage to exculpate himself.

Porfirii is chiefly sustained by his empty talk, which he can practice in any circumstances whatsoever. All he needs is an audience, and when he is finally deprived of that (with Evpraksiia's rebellion), he progresses naturally to its inward alternative of empty thought (*pustomyslie*), which gives him the freedom to create and rule over a world of his own fantasy. The transition from empty talk to empty thought is described in "Escheated," where the record of Porfirii's physical and mental decline begins. Up to this point he has had an unbroken run of successes. He has gained possession of the

Golovlyov estates and assisted in the elimination of most of his family. Unaffected by the rebuffs he receives from Arina Petrovna and Annin'ka (on her first return to Golovlyovo), he has, in "Illicit Family Joys," attained the peak of achievement by extracting himself from a seemingly inescapable situation with a consummate display of hypocrisy and verbal casuistry. But this is his last victory. No longer having anyone to dominate, he becomes a recluse living on his own fantasies, and the final degeneration of his personality begins.

The end of Porfirii caused Saltykov some difficulty and, as has been noted, not until four years after writing "Escheated" did he complete the final chapter. He made an early attempt to write a conclusion – "Haven Home," in which Porfirii was to fall victim to the designs of his cousin Galkina to marry him off to one of her daughters who would, on his death, gain possession of Golovlyovo – and no doubt in the meantime lead him a merry chase. He rightly abandoned this trivial solution; although it would have given Porfirii his comeuppance, its tone was not in keeping with that of the preceding chapters and it would have left unresolved the serious moral and psychological issues presented by Porfirii's character. Saltykov's contemporary readers took a keen interest in Porfirii, and one of them, Goncharov, the novelist and author of *Oblomov*, wrote to Saltykov about the prospective ending.[23] He expressed the view that Porfirii was a type incapable of ever realizing the truth of his situation and could never, therefore, end by committing suicide. In the event, Saltykov performed a *tour de force* by providing precisely the ending that Goncharov considered impossible. Porfirii *does* see the truth of his situation: in "The Reckoning," spurred by Annin'ka's savage indictments, his dormant conscience is stirred, and he seeks to escape its torments. Whether his nocturnal trek to Arina Petrovna's grave was an intended act of suicide is debatable, but the *idea* of killing himself was certainly present in those final pages of the novel when he insists on hearing again and again Annin'ka's account of Liubin'ka's suicide, and himself realizes that since natural death would not come to relieve him, "some act of force was required to expedite it." The revelation of Porfirii's conscience at the end is not, it must be said, an arbitrary contrivance of the author. It was Saltykov's conviction that in no human being could the human element be totally suppressed and extinguished. Human frailty and feeling were ultimately revealed in Arina Petrovna; it is the same with Porfirii. In fact, there are suggestions of flickerings of conscience in him in earlier chapters.[24] Then, in his prime, he was able to suppress these flickerings; in "The Reckoning," however, Porfirii – declining physically, mentally confused, and assailed by Annin'ka – can no longer resist the claims of conscience. In the end he realizes the futility of his life, the desolation he has caused, and his own isolation. Consciousness is the prerequisite of conscience, and in Porfirii the one leads naturally to the other.

Porfirii's character and the manner of his end have been the dominant themes of critical discussion of *The Golovlyovs* and have given rise to different views. There are two main matters of dispute: First, is Porfirii to be seen principally as a social phenomenon, a product of the society that bred him, or as an individual case of warped psychology? And second, what conclusions are we to draw from his change of heart at the end?

To an extent, certainly, Porfirii's character is determined by his belonging to the privileged landowning gentry. He suffers from the Golovlyovs' common disability of idleness, incapacity for useful activity, and hard drinking, referred to in "The Reckoning," that stems from their having been for generations cushioned, by privilege and economic security, from any *need* to engage in useful employment. Critics of the day pointed to the influence on Porfirii of his milieu and upbringing: the acquisitiveness inspired by the example of his mother, the empty copybook morality that was traditional among the unenlightened lesser gentry. He was compared to Chichikov, the roguish trickster in Gogol's *Dead Souls*, who had also been trained by example and precept to be submissive and ingratiating – and, at the same time, never to give a sucker an even break. One critic commended – perhaps ironically – Porfirii's consistency in adhering to a traditional set of moral values; it just happened that the values themselves were wrong. Soviet critics have mostly been categorical in answering the social question, insisting that Porfirii is not merely a product of his class but is in fact its quintessential embodiment, combining within himself all the characteristic vices of the "gentry exploiters."[25] This accords with their generally maintained view that the novel is to be seen first and foremost as a denunciation of the gentry.

It has to be said, though, that Porfirii is more than a historical figure, which this class-determined view would make him. His particular vices belong to him as an individual rather than as a member of a class (he is, after all, clearly distinct from the other Golovlyovs, who detest him). All the features that make Porfirii so singularly awful – his pleasure in tormenting others, his lack of human feeling, his hypocrisy, his pettifogging ways, his nauseating empty talk, his obsession with form, and his determined shunning of "reality" – can only be explained as stemming from some personal psychological malaise. Porfirii is a pathological case – a "boxed" figure, self-confined, incapable of relating normally to other people or to reality. His literary ancestors (no influence is suggested) are to be found in such misfit loners as Dostoevsky's Underground Man in *Zapiski iz podpol'ia* (*Notes from the Underground*) and Gogol's Akakii Akakievich, the government clerk in "Shinel' " ("The Overcoat"), who is so obsessed with form that he finds total fullfilment in his routine task of copying documents. As Golovin, writing in 1897, put it: "As a type, he [Porfirii] is completely individual and at the same time universal . . . [suffering from] a spiritual cancer that could infect a man of any circle. There are Judases [Iudushki] not only in Russia and not only in the gentry class."[26] It is indeed the "universality" of Porfirii as a type that places him among the classic figures of literature. Soviet commentators, although insisting that Porfirii's character is class-determined, also acknowledge him to be a universal type, giving particular emphasis to his role as hypocrite and traitor. In this they have followed the lead of Lenin, who freely applied the label of "Iudushka" to his political opponents (an indication of the impact Saltykov's work had on the intellectual younger generation of his time); Constitutional Democrats, Mensheviks, Trotsky, Kautsky were all "Iudushki." According to the Soviet line, the treachery and hypocrisy that Porfirii personified were inherited, after the decline of the gentry, by the new "exploiting class" (the bourgeoisie) and are (or were) to be found in our own times in the Western capitalist world.[27]

The second question – what we are to understand from the ending – has also aroused much discussion and some division of opinion. The division is broadly between prerevolutionary critics and those of the Soviet period. The "tragic pathos" in Porfirii's transformation from reviled villain to suffering human being is generally recognized. The difference is over what response this pathos should evoke. Earlier critics tended to see the awakening of Porfirii's conscience as providing a "moral" ending that reconciles Porfirii to the reader; Soviet critics, on the other hand, take a harsher view and emphasize the fact (stated, indeed, by Saltykov) that Porfirii's conscience brings him only pain and no hope of regeneration, punishment rather than purgation. In particular, they dismiss any suggestion that in referring to the story of Christ's Passion as a factor in the resolution of Porfirii's agony Saltykov was preaching the idea of Christian forgiveness for all.[28] Both views are supportable. Conscience does bring Porfirii torment rather than consolation (for such is the function of conscience). At the same time, and the ending *is* moral, since Porfirii's recognition of the sham of his own morality implies the existence of a better morality by which to live. To say that Porfirii is reconciled to the reader (or, as Protopopov claims, "rehabilitated" in his eyes)[29] goes perhaps further than might be accepted by some readers, who, after suffering through the book with Porfirii's victims, would be well content to see him damned unrepentant.

For a proper understanding of the ending it is important to consider the novel not in itself, but in the wider context of Saltykov's work as a whole. The role of conscience in bringing about a transformation of human life – of individuals as of societies – was for Saltykov crucial. It plays a significant part in works other than *The Golovlyovs* and in two works in particular, both similar to *The*

Golovlyovs as longer compositions with a coherent development. These are the mock chronicle of the town of Glupov – *Istoriia odnogo goroda* (*The History of a Town*, 1869–70) and the novel *Sovremennaia idilliia* (*A Contemporary Idyll*, 1877–83). At the end of *The History of a Town* the inhabitants of Glupov, who have from time immemorial passively suffered the tyranny of their lunatic governors, finally realize the folly of their submissiveness and *are ashamed*. *A Contemporary Idyll* ends similarly when the two heroes, renegade liberals who have stooped to every kind of baseness to demonstrate to the authorities that they are "well-intentioned," are visited by *Shame*. These works exemplify Saltykov's view that human dignity and decency can be attained by even the most abject of beings. The key to their attainment is consciousness and conscience. In all his works Saltykov's purpose was to bring society to an awareness of its condition, so that, with awareness and the consequent working of conscience, a better order might be created. No man, no society is beyond correction, and some inextinguishable spark of humanity exists in even the worst of men. It exists, too, in Porfirii and, though it is revealed too late, its presence is indicated and can be seen as an affirmation of Saltykov's belief in a better future world.[30]

The "class" factor as a determinant in forming Porfirii's character has already been mentioned. Porfirii, however he might dominate the novel, is, though, only one character. It is all the Golovlyovs – nine characters in three generations – with whom the novel is concerned, and it is in the generality of the family rather than in the particularity of Porfirii that its social import lies. The account Saltykov gives of the disintegration of this one family points to the broader implication of the disintegration of the gentry class as a whole. Contemporary critics remarked on the social typicality of the Golovlyovs. Skabichevskii, in his review of "Family Court," although he thought it "archeological" because it related to a "now bygone past" (i.e., pre-emancipation times), acknowledged nonetheless that it presented "true Russian characters" who manifested certain traits of the Russian "cultivated class" (i.e., the gentry) that still prevailed in the 1870s. "We are all of us flesh of their flesh and bone of their bone," he wrote. For the reviewer in *Molva*, the principal Golovlyovs were "products of a whole social stratum." Vvedenskii, writing in the 1880s, noted that characters such as the Golovlyovs were familiar figures in "our society." Saltykov himself clearly indicated the "class" factor of the novel. This was evident in the title he chose – <u>*Gospoda*</u> *Golovlyovy* – with its reference to the Golovlyovs as *masters* (see n. 1). Most important, he clearly stated the novel's social-historical import in the final chapter, where he gives a summary analysis of the origin and nature of the Golovlyov malaise. In this frequently quoted passage he speaks of the "seemingly ineluctable destiny" that hangs over certain families, particularly families of "the lower gentry, who, with no practical concerns, no involvement in life at large, and no significance as a directing force, at first . . . found shelter in serfdom, but who now, with no shelter whatsoever, live out their lives in decaying manor houses." The Golovlyovs, he goes on to say, had for several generations been debilitated by three factors: "idleness, incapacity for any activity whatsoever, and hard drinking." Most crucial of these was "idleness;" the other two were its consequences. With "the shelter of serfdom" they had had no *need* to be active in order to survive, thus idleness was the inevitable result. Serfdom, and the economic independence it gave to all but the most feckless, was the root cause of the Golovlyovs' condition. Serfdom, as well as imposing a monstrous injustice on the serfs, had also undermined the moral forces of their masters. Lacking the need to engage in any serious practical activity, they ceased to have the will or ability to do so, and devitalization and moral dissolution set in. The Golovlyovs' "hard drinking" was not itself a prime cause of their condition but merely "the inevitable conclusion to the general shambles of their lives."[31]

In light of this, it is not enough to claim *The Golovlyovs* as yet another condemnation of serfdom on the usual grounds of its injustice, exploitation, and cruelty (a view presented in some Soviet criticism, where the novel is described as "the death sentence on serfdom," etc.). Saltykov in his time had done his share of condemning these aspects of serfdom – in the grim story "Misha and Vania" (1863), for instance, which tells of two peasant boys who are driven to commit suicide by the cruelties of their mistress; but that particular horse was dead and scarcely needed further flogging.[32] In *The Golovlyovs* Saltykov condemns serfdom not so much for what it did to the serfs but for what it did to the masters, whom he shows to have been its moral victims.[33] It is they who have been spiritually corrupted and rendered unfit for life in any other form than that to which they were brought up. There are, true, a few incidental references in the novel to harsh treatment of the serfs, but for the most part the Golovlyov tyrants who oppress, exploit, and injure direct their oppression, exploitation, and injuring not at peasants but at members of their own family, their own sons and brothers. As an attack on serfdom, *The Golovlyovs* was not concerned with its well-attested inhumanities, which now belonged largely to the past, but with the moral and psychological distortion it had caused in the landowning class itself, the effects of which remained as a heritage in the present.

This should not of course be taken to indicate that Saltykov saw the landowning gentry as merely the victims of a historical process. His view of the class was consistently negative and, in his satires from the 1850s on, he showed how they had contributed to their own decline by their feckless incompetence, self-indulgence, and material self-interest. Their main social concern was the maintenance of their own privileges and enjoyment of the unearned benefits that derived from them. In *The Golovlyovs* we see even the passive Pavel stirring on his deathbed to calculate the income he expects from his investments, and Porfirii, in "Escheated," dreams of the proceeds he will receive from his estate, "from fines, usury, natural disasters, and the purchase of stocks and shares" – which together, Saltykov remarks, constituted "a whole . . . world embodying all the idle aspirations of a gentry landowner."

Saltykov recognized cultural gradations in the gentry. The Golovlyovs represent an extreme of brutal degradation and should not be taken as the "average" in Saltykov's perception of the class. An interesting contrast to the Golovlyovs is provided in another work that Saltykov wrote in the interval between "Escheated" (1876) and

"The Reckoning" (1880). This is *Ubezhishche Monrepo* (*The Refuge of Mon Repos*), written in 1878–79. It is a compact work of five chapters, ironic-elegiac in tone, in which the narrator – a "cultivated man" (*kul'turnyi chelovek*), which is Saltykov's mocking designation of the gentry – records his fate. Impoverished, unable to contend with the new conditions of the post-emancipation world, he takes refuge in his run-down manor house to live out his last days. He has all the weaknesses of his class, but he is a decent enough man, bewildered by the collapse of his world and defenseless against the harsh realities of the new age. These realities, for him, are represented by the brash kulak entrepreneur Razuvaev, who is set on buying him out of his estate, and the local police agent, who suspects him – because of his vaguely liberal past and present ambiguous situation – of being politically unreliable (*neblagonamerennyi*). Beset as he is by these crude forces, the "cultivated man" engages the reader's sympathy; at the same time the reader is left in no doubt that the "cultivated man" is himself – because of his past easy-going indolence – largely responsible for his plight. *The Refuge of Mon Repos* is, in fact, only a variation, in a subdued minor key, on the theme of gentry decline that *The Golovlyovs* presents in starker form.

Because Saltykov records the extinction of the Golovlyov family, the novel might be regarded as a parting shot at a now spent class. In fact, though, he does not see the end of the Golovlyovs as quite the end of the gentry: the social features they represent do not pass away with them, and within the gentry class there are still pockets of vitality. The Golovlyovs, Saltykov explains in "The Reckoning," were one of "the great multitude of [lesser gentry] families" whose "ineluctable destiny" it was to be unsuccessful (*neudachlivyi*, from *udacha*, which has the sense of "good fortune" as well as "success"). There are, though, other families of the same social class whose destiny it is to succeed. They have the right connections, do the right things, their sons make successful careers, their daughters make successful marriages, and all prosper. Basically they are no different, no more worthy, than the Golovlyovs (Porfirii excepted!) – they are just luckier. The "success" they achieve is unmerited and, in Saltykov's eyes, of no intrinsic value, since it is success achieved in the specious and corrupt world of those "who assume they possess an inborn right to lifelong junketing" – a world that was a regular object of scorn in Saltykov's satires. That world continues to exist. In rural Russia, too, the landowning gentry are not finished. Though many of them failed in the new conditions created by the emancipation, others prospered. Even the Golovlyovs, though morally in decline, maintain their material position: after the emancipation, Arina Petrovna continues to add to the Golovlyov property (to the benefit of Porfirii), and Porfirii, for all his pettifogging bureaucratic management, holds his place as "the biggest landowner of the district." In the book's final paragraph, note is taken of the keen interest with which cousin Galkina has been following events in Golovlyovo – a clear indication that the breed of tough, rapacious gentry landowners is not yet extinct.[34] *The Golovlyovs*, while giving clear notice of the decline of the gentry landowning class, makes it clear too that the decline is not yet terminal.

Saltykov's dominating concern in *The Golovlyovs* is with the family and with relations within the family. Relations between the Golovlyovs, as masters, and their peasants are not a major theme, but the peasants, as the foundation of the Golovlyovo economy and as a moral force, are a significant background presence. Passing reference is made in "Family Court" to the harsh treatment of serfs before the emancipation, when Arina Petrovna summarily orders Ivan Mikhailych to be conscripted (to twenty-five years of military service!) for showing kindness to her unfavored son Stepan; reference is again made in "Illicit Family Joys," when Arina Petrovna recalls her punishment of errant peasant girls by forcing them into marriage with elderly unsuitable partners. Porfirii, as master in the new times, has no such seigneurial rights; his abuse of the peasants is strictly "according to the law," which he uses to the full – capitalizing on their poverty by making them loans at extortionate rates of interest, confiscating their hens that stray on his land, imposing a fine for a felled tree. More important, though, than these familiar indications of the abuse of peasants by their masters is the moral contrast that the peasants, with their simple virtues, provide to the degenerate Golovlyovs. The only acts of decency recorded in the novel are performed by peasants: Ivan Mikhailych, who shelters Stepan Golovlyov in Moscow, who solicitously escorts him to Golovlyovo and discreetly gives him money; the Golovlyovo peasants who look with pity on the returned prodigal; the Dubrovino peasant who scrupulously gives to Porfirii the small debt he had owed to the now dead Pavel; the Pogorelka peasants who show warmth and affection for Annin'ka (and are hostile to Porfirii and his Golovlyovo ways). The same humanity is shown by Evpraksiia (not a peasant but, as the daughter of a minor church servitor, of the lower orders), even to her tormentor Porfirii when she sees his wretched state in "Escheated." In all these examples we see the peasants as morally superior to their masters. More significant, however, than the contrast these individuals provide is the "symbolic" peasant – the "black dot" Stepan and Arina Petrovna see toiling in the distance as they gaze aimlessly from their windows. In the first chapter Stepan realizes the truth about his idle, wasted life (in the last chapter, Saltykov will generalize this truth in his diagnosis of the Golovlyov malaise): Watching the "black dots" at their work outside, he contrasts his own lassitude and dejection with their endless toil as they "struggle to fashion something, make it secure and strong"; he is not concerned with whether this "something" is worth their toil, "but he knew well that even these nameless dots were immeasurably superior to him, that he could not even struggle, and he had nothing to make secure and strong." The image of the "black dot" suggests a view of the peasantry as an insensate mass, but this mass is productive (note the abundant provisions supplied to Golovlyovo) and the elemental life it leads has its own logic. Not that Saltykov romanticizes the peasant lot; in "The Niece" he speaks of the peasants' life of toil as "an inborn obligation" to which they are "condemned by some accursed original sin." Still, the implication of the peasant references, individual and general, seems to be that Saltykov saw the peasantry as a moral and physical force, which, released from its bondage of toil and ignorance, would play its part in some future new society – to which, by contrast, the enfeebled gentry could contribute nothing.

The Golovlyovs, which has been described – not unfairly – as "the darkest, the gloomiest, and the most intimidating novel in Russian literature,"[35] is not entirely without hope. It is there in the aspirations of the young to escape from Golovlyovo to a "better life," in Annin'ka's (and Evpraksiia's) resistance to Porfirii's tyranny, in Arina Petrovna's tardy enlightenment, and in the stirrings of Porfirii's conscience. It is also suggested, obscurely, in the mysterious power of the "black dots." It is likely that readers will be more impressed (and depressed) by the body count than by these thin rays of hope, but they are there, placed with hesitant conviction by the "skeptical optimist"[36] author.

The character of *The Golovlyovs* as a novel was determined by the way in which it was written. It is not a novel of intrigue and there is no plot to be resolved at the end. Each chapter tells a distinct story (*rasskaz* in Russian, the word Saltykov used to refer to the individual chapters while they were in preparation); each is an episode of Golovlyov family life that is complete in itself. The title Saltykov first considered for the work was, not unfittingly, *Episodes from the History of a Family*.[37] After the first chapter, in which Stepan and Arina Petrovna are the principal characters, Porfirii occupies center stage, revealing episode by episode the full horror of his nature in his confrontations with Pavel ("Kith and Kin"), Arina Petrovna ("Kith and Kin," "Family Scores"), his sons ("Family Scores"), Annin'ka ("The Niece"), and Evpraksiia ("Illicit Family Joys," "Escheated"). The confrontations end with his isolation in "Escheated" but resume in the final chapter with Annin'ka's return, which leads to his end. Only in the last two chapters is there anything that might be called "development" – Porfirii's decline and his final change of heart. Some events are linked in different chapters (the consequences of Petia's rejected plea in "Family Scores" recounted in "The Niece," for example), and chapter openings make it clear that the story of the Golovlyovs is resuming. In other respects each episode tells its own story and has its own climax. The episodes are given in chronological order, spaced at intervals of from ten years to a single year or less. The one episode given out of sequence is "Illicit Family Joys" (Evpraksiia's pregnancy precedes Arina Petrovna's death, which is reported in "The Niece"), but there is a structural logic to this: having previously worked through the members of his family, Porfirii now turns his attention to a nonfamily victim, Evpraksiia, and his misuse of her leads naturally to his decline which starts in "Escheated." Continuity is more marked in the last three chapters than in the others.

Within each chapter there is an alternation of "analytical" passages and narrative (much of the latter consisting of conversations). In this, Saltykov follows the pattern he regularly used in his sketches – discursive introduction followed by live illustration of his theme. For all the characters there are extended passages describing their daily routines, their thoughts, their emotions, and into these the author frequently interjects his own comments and reflections.[38] Some critics have found these discursive and descriptive sections ponderous and long-winded, but they are intrinsic to the Golovlyov theme and a necessary guide to the reader's understanding; it may be said, too, that the formal mode in which they are written contributes significantly to the serious tone of the novel.

Not only in these analytical passages is the author's voice heard. He is a constant presence in the novel, frequently making caustic comments and ironic asides on the characters and their actions. He does not conceal his attitude toward them, particularly his antipathy toward Porfirii. Repeatedly he refers to him with the family nickname "Judas" and damns him with bald statements, such as "he was infinitely ignorant, a pettifogger, a liar" or "[Arina Petrovna's curse] restrained him from many shabby deeds (of which he was such a masterly performer)." This censorious tone and the frequent passing ironies (for example, the family gathering to condemn Stepan is described as a "happy reunion") are part and parcel of Saltykov's manner as a satirist; contrary to the view that Saltykov was abandoning satire in *The Golovlyovs*, the novel provides ample evidence of the author's satirical bent. Saltykov the novelist, like Saltykov the satirist, is concerned with exposing a social ill and, in doing so, plays the role of critic and moralist. Ridicule and caricature, the satirist's favorite weapons, are certainly present in the work, especially in the many comic features in the portrayal of Porfirii: his exaggerated false piety (the comedy of which is recognized by his sons, who mimic him), his footling talk, and his set-piece "comedies" (*komedii* is Saltykov's word)[39] – the "solicitous brother" act at Pavel's deathbed, lamenting over his grave (foreseen exactly by Arina Petrovna), the ritual leave-taking "as kith and kin" of departing visitors. These aspects of Porfirii's conduct are undoubtedly comic and satirical, though, of course, overshadowed by the grim reality that underlies his pretense. Among the Golovlyovs it is Porfirii who is the subject of satirical treatment; outside the confines of Golovlyovo there are a number of incidental references to social types and institutions that recall the general tenor of Saltykov's principal work as a writer of satirical sketches. (A summary of these references is provided in section 2 ["Satirical Elements in *The Golovlyovs*"].[40] Also considered in that section are the means Saltykov employs to create the novel's powerful stylistic stamp, discussed in some detail in the articles by Ehre, Foote, and Kramer.)

Though *The Golovlyovs*, being a novel, is not typical of Saltykov's work in terms of genre, it is certainly typical in its main characteristics. It is concerned with a particular problem of contemporary society – the state of the gentry class – and delivers a powerful indictment. The milieu and characters are faithfully portrayed; although the colors may be more somber than those of everyday reality, the picture itself, informed as it is by the author's profound experience and observation of Russian life, is authentic. If Porfirii's portrayal as a double-dyed villain has strained some readers' credulity, remember that Saltykov made frequent use of grotesque images in his satires – the grotesque, he claimed, did not invalidate but served to convey the true essence of a phenomenon. Also typical is Saltykov's manner of writing, which shows his impressive command of the different linguistic registers of the Russian language – formal and skillfully emotive in the authorial (analytical and descriptive) passages, richly colloquial and varied in the speech of the characters, who are all precisely individualized by their manner of speaking. Above all, the typicality of *The Golovlyovs* lies in its moral seriousness and humane concern for the betterment of men as individuals and social beings. All Saltykov's work – including his brightest comic satires[41] – was motivated by this concern. He had a deadly eye for the various forms of corruption that infected his own society, and he exposed these negative aspects with all the power of his formidable literary talent. Criticism was his stock in trade, but he criticized not from cynicism or misanthropy but from a genuine desire to improve the human lot. If he was appalled by the indignity and wretchedness of man, it was because he was concerned for man's dignity and well-being. It is this humane feeling that underlies the dismal tale of the Golovlyov family.

The first criticism of *The Golovlyovs* appeared in reviews of its individual chapters as they were published in *NF*. The early chapters were generally well received and it was noted with approval that Saltykov, in departing from his familiar satirical manner, had revealed new aspects of his talent (e.g., Skabichevskii; see section 2). A few voiced reservations, claiming that Saltykov should stick to his satirical last, and found fault with his long-winded interventions and lack of objectivity, especially in his portrayal of Porfiii (e.g., the reviewer of "Family Scores" in *Molva*[42] and V. V. Markov on "Escheated" in *Sankt-Peterburgskie vedomosti*).[43] Already in these piecemeal journal reviews the major issues of the novel were defined, with emphasis being placed on (1) its social relevance and (2) the significance of Porfirii. The interpretation of Porfirii's character became, of course, a more complex issue after publication of "The Reckoning" in 1880, and of the whole novel in a separate edition. The various opinions on the "social" and "Porfirii" questions have already been considered in the discussion of the novel's themes. The accuracy of Saltykov's social account was attested by contemporary critics (who were well placed to judge the issue), though there was some division of view on whether the picture of rural gentry society was actual or merely historical. Judgments on Porfirii and his fate in "The Reckoning" generally followed the humanitarian line. E. Solov'ëv noted that there was reconciliation with Porfirii in the end because the human element in him had, after all, prevailed.[44] M. A. Protopopov, as mentioned earlier, considered Porfirii to be "rehabilitated" for the reader by his repentance and saw in the ending of the novel "the triumph of a higher moral truth."[45] A. I. Vvedenskii took a not dissimilar line, regarding the finale as "a call not to despair and disbelief in the future, but to a rational understanding of life and to the struggle for all that is good and beautiful."[46] The general tendency, was then, clearly to see the problem of Porfirii as a moral, rather than a social one − a view also implicit in K. F. Golovin's declaration that Porfirii was a "universal" figure, one who might occur in any society in any age.[47]

The first decade or so after Saltykov's death in 1889 was a period when stock was taken of his total literary achievement. There was then some waning of critical interest in Saltykov's works, as the issues on which he wrote lost their topical savor, and the next thirty years saw little of significance added to the literature on *The Golovlyovs*, except perhaps for Kranikhfel'd's publication in 1914 of the fragment of "Haven Home" and the balanced assessment he gave of the novel as a whole.[48] *The Golovlyovs*, however, was served by the passage of time, since it increasingly stood out as a work that remained accessible to the general reader, which was not so in the case of most of Saltykov's other works.

Interest in Saltykov received fresh impetus in the 1930s, when the author was admitted into the pantheon of prerevolutionary writers approved by the Soviet literary authorities and was treated accordingly. The study of Saltykov (termed *shchedrinovedenie* in Russian) flourished, and a stream of critical books and articles, memoirs, documents, and so on, followed, as well as editions of his works (the first systematically, if tendentiously, edited *Collected Works* was published in twenty volumes, 1933–41). Saltykov's appeal to the Soviet establishment was understandable: although he held to no particular political ideology and was by no means a revolutionary (the Soviet claim that "Saltykov is one of us" ["*Saltykov – nash*"] was a patent exaggeration), he had been a hard-hitting critic of the old regime and was therefore claimed as an ally by the new. The revived interest in his work and the scholarly attention it received were beneficial. In the last sixty years much valuable work has been done, most notably in the achievements of S. A. Makashin, who produced a definitive four-volume biography of the writer and oversaw the best edition of his works (*Sobranie sochinenii v dvadtsati tomakh* [Moscow, 1965–1977]). There was, though, the disadvantage (common to all literary criticism of the Soviet period) that attitudes to Saltykov's work were largely prescribed (or at least, circumscribed) by ideological considerations. Assessment of *The Golovlyovs* was affected by this, with dogmatic emphasis given to its being primarily a denunciation of the gentry class and to the claim that Porfirii was essentially a product of that class. This approved view of the novel was firmly maintained in standard works on Saltykov by various authors writing from the 1930s to the 1960s, such as El'sberg, Kirpotin, and Goriachkina.[49] It also underlies the assessments found in the more scholarly and judicious studies of Bushmin and Pokusaev.[50] The books by the authors mentioned all deal with Saltykov's work as a whole and allot not more than a chapter to *The Golovlyovs*. Two short monographs devoted solely to the novel appeared in 1962 and 1975, one by K. N. Grigor'ian (*Roman M. E. Saltykova-Shchedrina "Gospoda Golovlëvy"*) and the other by Pokusaev ("*Gospoda Golovlëvy" M. E. Saltykova-Shchedrina*). The latter is an expanded version of the chapter on *The Golovlyovs* in his book *Revoliutsionnaia satira*. Grigor'ian's is an original and useful study that breaks out of the repetitive mold of most modern commentary on the novel. He concentrates on three features only ("The Psychological Aspect," "Comparisons, Portraiture," and "Landscape") and deals with each in greater depth and detail than is found elsewhere. Both authors maintain the priority of milieu in the formation of Porfirii's character and see his end as retribution rather than reconciliation. The two most recent general books on Saltykov, by prominent *shchedrinisty* of the second post-revolutionary generation, are those of D. Nikolaev and V. V. Prozorov.[51] Both books are intended for students' use and are notably more objective and original in their assessment of *The Golovlyovs* than some of the earlier and larger studies. Of many articles on *The Golovlyovs*, mention should be made of that by I. B. Pavlova (1975), which argues in favor of a "moral" view of the ending.[52]

Apart from books concerned with the content of Saltykov's work, two major studies on style and language have appeared in Russia: Ia. El'sberg, *Stil' Shchedrina* (1940) and A. I. Efimov, *Iazyk satiry Saltykova-Shchedrina* (1953). Both take an overall approach to their subject and, although they offer useful material for the study of *The Golovlyovs*, the absence of indexes makes it difficult to locate what is relevant.

English-language criticism of *The Golovlyovs* is slight in quantity, contained in a single book (Strelsky's *Saltykov and the Russian Squire*) and a few articles. The 1931 Duddington translation established the novel's place among the foreign classics and created some – but not much – interest among the nonspecialist literary fraternity. The most significant product of this interest was Pritchett's essay of 1946 (see section 2). Articles in academic journals followed only in the 1960s and 1970s (Foote, Kramer, Todd, and Ehre; all but Todd's article appear in section 2). Although small in number, these studies, like Pritchett's essay, have done something to broaden the scope of the novel's assessment. The social-historical aspect, repetitively discussed in Russian criticism, is refreshingly avoided (in any case it was comprehensively examined by Strelsky), and attention has been focused on Porfirii – in a psychological rather than social-moral context – and on features of the novel as a literary work (form, parodic elements, relation with non-Russian works). On the debated question of the end of Porfirii, the attitude of those Western writers who have considered it has tended to the humanitarian rather than the punitive view. The view of *The Golovlyovs* as parody (reversal of conventional family relationships, the "anti-hero" Porfirii) has been given some prominence, and a corrective word might be appropriate: although *The Golovlyovs* may be *read* as parody, one should keep firmly in mind that Saltykov was inspired to write the novel not by a desire to score polemical points off previous writers on the family theme, but to make a serious statement about the condition of contemporary society and to exorcise his own experience of family life.

———

There have been seven English translations of *The Golovlyovs* to date. The first two appeared in 1916 (trans. Athelstan Ridgeway, London) and 1917 (trans. A. Yarmolinsky, New York). Ridgeway's is an unsatisfactory version, truncated and often inaccurate. Yarmolinsky's translation is accurate and readable, but in the interests of readability the translator made free with Saltykov's text, introducing new divisions (thirty-six chapters in seven "Books"), recasting paragraphs and sentences, and compressing many longer passages, which inevitably resulted in the loss of some essential features of the original. Never reprinted, these translations are of little account today.

Natalie Duddington's translation (London, 1931) is a commendable version and, as the only translation available for many years, was reprinted several times under different imprints: New York: Macmillan, 1931; London: Dent-Dutton, 1934; London: Heron Books, 1968; and Westport, Conn.: Hyperion 1977. It has also been issued twice, with some modification – and no acknowledgment of Duddington as translator – in Russia as *Judas Golovlyov*, edited by Olga Shartse (Moscow: Foreign Languages Publishing House, 1957), and as *The Golovlyovs*, translated (!) by Olga Shartse (Moscow: Progress Publishers, 1975).

The next two translations appeared in the United States. Andrew R. MacAndrew's version (with an afterword by William E. Harkins [New York: New American Library, 1961]) is, like that of Yarmolinsky, accurate but compressed. The result is a good layman's version, although again lacking some of the stylistic stamp of the original. Samuel D. Cioran's translation (Ann Arbor, Mich.: Ardis, 1977) gives the full text, but the English style, inconsistent and often infelicitous, does not convincingly match the various levels of Salt-ykov's language – and it is not always accurate.

The most recent translations are those of I. P. Foote (Oxford: Oxford University Press, 1986) and Ronald Wilks (Harmondsworth: Penguin, 1988). Of my own translation I can only say that it attempts to convey as well as possible the text in the manner in which Saltykov wrote it; that it does not do full justice to the original I am well aware. Wilks's version is reliable, reads well, and competently matches the different stylistic modes employed in the novel.

Of the five translations most likely to be available, the best for students' use are those of Duddington, Foote, and Wilks. They are full translations and may be fairly rated as more satisfactory than Cioran's version. The general reader who does not wish to read Saltykov's every word can well turn to MacAndrew's translation.

NOTES

1. The title has been variously rendered by translators, most often as *The Golovlyovs* or *The Golovlyov Family*; Yarmolinsky (1917) called it *A Family of Noblemen*; the Moscow Foreign Languages Publishing House version (1957) titled it *Judas Golovlyov* after the principal character. The Russian *gospodin* (plural *gospoda*), used with a surname, may be the neutrally polite "mister." It has, though, also the meaning of "master" in relation to subordinates, and this nuance is certainly present, with some ironic implication, in Saltykov's title. Something like *The Masters of Golovlyovo* would convey this, but perhaps might be too specific a resolution of the ambiguity. Yarmolinsky may have intended to catch this nuance with his *A Family of Noblemen*.

2. "Well-intentioned" was used in Saltykov's day with particular reference to political conformity.

3. The chapters in *The Golovlyovs* have titles (as in the journal text) and are unnumbered. They will be referred to as follows: "Family Court" ("Semeinyi sud"), "Kith and Kin" ("Po-rodstvennomu"), "Family Scores" ("Semeinye itogi"), "The Niece" ("Plemiannushka"), "Illicit Family Joys" ("Nedozvolennye semeinye radosti"), "Escheated" ("Vymorochnyi"), and "The Reckoning" ("Raschet"). "Escheated," which is the literal translation

of *vymorochnyi*, is a now more or less obsolete legal term used of an estate that reverts to a larger domain when the heirs of succession run out. (The title "Entailed," which occurs in some translations, is inaccurate; it is used of property that can change hands only by inheritance, not by sale, gift, etc.) "Escheated" has the advantage of being literal but also has disadvantages: first, most readers will have to look it up in a dictionary, and, second, it does not have the ready association of moribundity contained in *vymorochnyi* (cf. the cognate verb *vymeret'* [to die out]). Saltykov's use of it in respect to a person (Porfirii) is unusual but clear in its meaning.

4. See the relevant extracts in section 3, letters 8 and 9.

5. See section 3, letter 6.

6. For details of "Haven Home," see section 3.

7. For footnotes to the journal text of "[Illicit] Family Joys," see section 3.

8. For one such passage, see section 3.

9. "Reshenie," the original title of the chapter, means "decision," "(re)solution," and may have been intended as an echo of the same word used at the very end of the novel when Porfirii makes the "decision" to visit his mother's grave. In the sense of "resolution" it could equally well refer to the resolution of Porfirii's situation. The change to "Raschet" is significant and appropriate: it introduces the idea of moral reckoning and the settling of accounts, with a suggestion, too, of "retribution."

10. Letter to E. I. Utin, 2 January 1881 (M. E. Saltykov-Shchedrin, *Sobranie sochinenii v dvadtsati tomakh* (henceforth, *SS*) (Moscow, 1965–77), 19[1]: 194).

11. N. A. Belogolovyi, "Iz vospominanii o M. E. Saltykove," in *M. E. Saltykov-Shchedrin v vospominaniiakh sovremennikov* (Moscow, 1975), 2: 264. For the Saltykov family, see also the biography of Makashin (see select bibliography in this volume) and E. Makarova, "O real'nykh istochnikakh 'Gospod Golovlëvykh' ('Semeinyi sud')," *Literaturnyi kritik* (Moscow, nos. 5–6, (1939): 103–14.

12. The similarities between Arina Petrovna and Ol'ga Mikhailovna are many: her domineering nature and relations with her children, her business acumen and achievements in enlarging the family property (Ol'ga Mikhailovna's purchase of the Zaozer'e estate in 1830 is echoed in Arina Petrovna's acquisition of Dubrovino), her having nine children, her burial at Khot'kov, and so on.

13. Nikolai, like Stepan, was the black sheep of the family. After attend-

ing Moscow University, he drifted through various occupations, served in the militia raised for the Crimea, and died at the age of thirty-five in 1856 (the approximate year of Stepan's death).

14. "My evil genius" was how Saltykov described Dmitrii in a letter to his mother (9 March 1873, *SS*, 18 [2]: 137). References to Dmitrii in Saltykov's letters could easily be read as relating to Porfirii Golovlyov, for example: "Any matter that might be settled in two words he goes on and on about ad infinitum as if on purpose . . . his only way of acting is to perform little dirty tricks. And is it not finally sickening – this hypocrisy, this perpetual mask that the man puts on as he then prays to God with one hand and casts aspersions with the other" (letter to O. M. Saltykova, 22 April 1873, *SS*, 18 [2]: 143–44). Although Dmitrii was the main inspiration for Porfirii, certain aspects of Porfirii's character can be related to Saltykov's father, Evgraf Vasil'evich, who was excessively pious and obsessed with church ritual. Although there is a connection between Evgraf Vasil'evich and Vladimir Mikhailovich Golovlyov in respect to the subordinate role they both played in family affairs, their resemblance is less close than that between other Golovlyovs and their Saltykov prototypes.

15. Quoted from notes of Saltykov's correspondence with A. M. Unkovskii; the letters themselves were destroyed. See *SS*, 18 (2): 352.

16. An 1863 sketch entitled "Semeinoe schast'e" ("Family Happiness") had shown a similar family circle – the Volovitinovs – with a domineering mother, three sons similar to the Golovlyov sons, and two orphaned grandchildren. Lighthearted rather than grim, "Family Happiness" can be seen as a preliminary sketch for the novel (in fact, this sketch, though of an earlier date, was included in *Well-Intentioned Speeches* when the cycle was published separately without the Golovlyov episodes). A more serious and detailed reflection of the Saltykov family is found in Saltykov's last major work, *Poshekhonskaia starina* (*Old Times in Poshekhon'e*), written in 1887–89. In its presentation of the Zatrapeznyi family this work has much in common with *The Golovlyovs*, though it is broader in scope than the novel and goes beyond inner family relations. It also relates to the pre-emancipation period and touches on some of the more harrowing aspects of serfdom.

17. Belogolovyi, *Iz vospominanii o M. E. Saltykove*, 2:264.

18. "Empty talk" is a somewhat cumbrous rendering of *pustoslovie*, but it maintains the thematic reference to "emptiness" that occurs in the parallel words *pustomyslie* and *pustoutrobie*. A common translation is "prattle," but

prattle is aimless and *harmless*: Porfirii's *pustoslovie* has more serious overtones, suggestive of the hollowness of his words and of his personality.

19. The standard form for "Judas" in Russian is "Iuda." Porfirii's nickname is in the derived form of "Iudushka," which conveys the idea of "petty Judas" – a "sneak" rather than a "betrayer." The nickname "Candid Lad" (*otkrovennyi mal'chik*) may be a reference to Porfirii's "candor" in snitching on his siblings to his mother; alternatively, it may be – given his secretive ways – simply ironic.

20. Pokusaev observes that contemporary statistics showed that 70 percent of the children admitted to foundlings' homes died within two years (E. Pokusaev, *"Gospoda Golovlyëvy" M. E. Saltykova-Shchedrina* [Moscow: Khudozhestvennaia literatura, 1975], 51).

21. For example, "The author [Saltykov] has drawn Judas – a Russian Tartuffe – with great thoroughness" (V. S. Solov'ëv in *Russkii mir*, no. 147 (1876), reprinted in Denisiuk, *Kriticheskaia literatura* [for full reference, see select bibliography] 3: 116–23).

22. In "Family Scores" Porfirii's obsession with form is related to his "thirty years" in the civil service, where he had "acquired all the habits and cherished aspirations of the confirmed bureaucrat." The petty orderliness of bureaucratic procedures would certainly appeal to him, but it is to his nature rather than his bureaucratic experience that his formalism is attributable. Information given in the novel about Porfirii's service career is sparse: in "The Niece" he is said to have had no living contacts in the "dead world" of the bureaucracy; in "Escheated" he mentally pays off old scores on colleagues who were promoted ahead of him. His claim to the title "Excellency" (in "Kith and Kin") suggests he had attained the fourth grade in the Table of Ranks (the lowest which gave that title) – this would be compatible at least with his length of service, if not, perhaps, with his seemingly modest achievements (no bar, though, then as now, to promotion in government service).

23. See section 3, letter 11.

24. Three moments suggest the stirring of human feeling in Porfirii: in "Family Scores," where a "muffled voice" within him questions the appropriateness of his action vis-à-vis Petia; in "Illicit Family Joys" he experiences "something like conscience" during his dilemma over Evpraksiia's pregnancy; and, in the same chapter, he shows a spark of paternal feeling – immediately suppressed – when Ulita confronts him with his newborn son.

25. Bushmin notes astutely that Porfirii Golovlyov is a compound of the defects of the main characters Gogol presented in *Dead Souls* – having the miserliness of Pliushkin, the rapacity of Sobakevich, the niggardliness of Korobochka, the sugary effusiveness of Manilov, the lying of Nozdrëv, and the ingenuity of Chichikov (A. S. Bushmin, *Satira Saltykova-Shchedrina* [Moscow-Leningrad: Akademiia nauk, 1959], 185).

26. In Denisiuk, *Kriticheskaia literatura*, 5:271 (an extract from Golovin is printed in section 2).

27. See, for example, Pokusaev's declaration: "The denunciatory point of Saltykov's novel is today directed against the capitalist world. The policy of the ideologists of imperialism and anti-communism is, after all, filled with mendacious Judas-playing (*iudushkinoi igry*) at democracy and hypocritical preaching of the pretended humane ideals of the so-called free society" (E. Pokusaev, "*Gospoda Golovlëvy*" *M. E. Saltykova-Shchedrina* [Moscow: Khudozhestvennaia literatura, 1975], 114). On one occasion, at least, the image was turned against the Soviets themselves – by Edmond Jaloux in his introduction to a French translation of *The Golovlyovs* published in 1922 (the passage in question is cited by Strelsky in the extract from his book printed in section 2).

28. The Eastertide setting of the final scene with its reference to the story of Christ's Passion fulfills more than one function. It intensifies the mood of solemn seriousness of the novel's climax; dramatically, it serves as the final impulse to Porfirii to act out his repentance; thematically, it emphasizes the common bond of the human condition (all are affected by the Passion story, serfs and masters); and it does (pace the Soviet commentators) point to the possibility of forgiveness for all: the Gospel account of the Crucifixion contains Christ's prayer for His executioners, "Father, forgive them; for they know not what they do" (*Luke*, 23:34), which can be related, at least indirectly, to Saltykov's view that *consciousness* of their wrong ways will bring men to lead better lives. Though not a religious man, Saltykov recognized the power of Christ as a symbol of truth and justice (see, in his *Fables*, "Easter Night" and "A Christmas Story"). Speaking through the narrator in *Old Times in Poshekhon'e*, Saltykov recalls (in chapter 5) the deep effect the Lenten Gospel readings had on him in childhood, revealing to him the need for social justice.

29. For Protopopov's views on Porfirii, see section 2.

30. Saltykov referred to the importance of shame in a letter of 25 No-

vember 1876 to P. V. Annenkov: "For the present-day Russian it is hard to live and even rather shaming. Not many yet feel shame, however, and most, even the people of so-called culture, live simply without shame at all. Arousing shame is at present the most rewarding theme for developing in literature, and I try, as possibility allows, to touch on it" (*SS*, 19 [1]: 33). For a discussion of the question, see V. A. Mysliakov, "Tema 'styda' v tvorchestve Saltykova-Shchedrina" (The Theme of "Shame" in the Work of Saltykov-Shchedrin), *Russkaia literatura*, no. 3 (1973): 132–39.

31. These deficiencies of the Golovlyovs are, of course, the same as those from which that earlier breed of ineffectuals, the celebrated "superfluous men," had suffered – the gentry heroes of Pushkin (Onegin), Lermontov (Pechorin), Turgenev (Rudin, Lavretskii, and others), Goncharov (Oblomov). They are different from the Golovlyovs only in their higher level of intellect and social culture, their propensity to self-analysis – and their apparent avoidance of recourse to hard liquor.

32. Later, in *Old Times in Poshekhon'e*, which is set in pre-emancipation times, Saltykov did return to the theme of the cruelties inflicted by masters on their serfs.

33. Moral corruption could affect serfs, too – as seen in the example of Ulita, the Golovlyov servant, who has become soured and vicious as a result of her frustrated efforts to gain power by servility to her masters.

34. In Galkina, this breed finds – after Arina Petrovna – another *female* representative; a further strong woman landowner, Mashen'ka Velichkina, is the subject of two sketches included in *Well-Intentioned Speeches*: "Kuzina Mashen'ka" ("Cousin Mashen'ka") and "Nepochtitel'nyi Koronat" ("Disrespectful Koronat"). These hard, resourceful women are no doubt a sign of the lasting impression made on Saltykov by his mother. In general, Saltykov's experience with women was uncomfortable, since, as well as a domineering mother, he had a demanding and unsympathetic wife (in his latter years he spoke of "the hell of family life"). We might note that the only serious opposition Porfirii encounters comes from women – Arina Petrovna, Annin'ka, Evpraksiia, and Ulita.

35. [R. D. Charques], "A Russian Satirist," *Times Literary Supplement*, 22 October 1931, 810.

36. "Skeptical optimism" is the phrase used by S. A. Makashin to characterize Saltykov's philosophy in his introduction to the 1975 Moscow translation of *The Golovlyovs*.

37. See section 3, letter 6.

38. Extended passages on the various characters occur as follows: Arina Petrovna in "Family Court," "Kith and Kin," and "Family Scores"; her children collectively in "Family Court"; Stepan in "Family Court"; Pavel in "Kith and Kin"; Porfirii in "Family Scores," "The Niece," "Illicit Family Joys," "Escheated," and "The Reckoning"; Annin'ka in "The Niece" and "The Reckoning"; Evpraksiia in "Illicit Family Joys"; and Ulita in "Illicit Family Joys."

39. For a discussion of these *komedii*, see D. Nikolaev, *M. E. Saltykov-Shchedrin, zhizn' i tvorchestvo* (Moscow: Detskaia literatura, 1985), 181–85.

40. For satire in the novel, see also Karl D. Kramer's article "Satiric Form in Saltykov's *Gospoda Golovlevy*," reprinted in section 2.

41. No assessment of Saltykov could be wider of the mark than that of the radical critic Dmitrii Pisarev in his tendentious article "Tsvety nevinnogo iumora" (The Flowers of Innocent Humor), published in 1864. In it he decried Saltykov's writings as being "laughter for laughter's sake" and denied them any serious significance.

42. *Molva*, no.14 (1876) (Denisiuk, *Kriticheskaia literatura*, 2:55–63). The review in general was favorable, but the reviewer took exception to the lack of objectivity in the portrayal of Porfirii and of the intrusive "authorial explanations" in the text.

43. See the extract in section 2.

44. E. Solov'ev, "Kholopy i kholopstvo v satire Shchedrina" (Bond serfs and serfdom in Shchedrin's satire), from "Semidesiatye gody: M. E. Saltykov," *Zhizn'*, no.4 (1899): (1) (Denisiuk, *Kriticheskaia literatura*, 5:334–63).

45. See the extract in section 2.

46. See the extract in section 2.

47. See the extract in section 2.

48. Vl. [V. P.] Kranikhfel'd, "Novaia ekskursiia v Golovlëvo. (K 25-letiiu godovshchiny smerti M. E. Saltykova-Shchedrina)" (A fresh excursion to Golovlëvo. [for the 25th anniversary of the death of M. E. Saltykov-Shchedrin]), *Russkoe bogatstvo*, no. 4 (1914): 38–52.

49. El'sberg, *Saltykov-Shchedrin, zhizn' i tvorchestvo* (1953); Kirpotin, *Mikhail Evgrafovich Saltykov-Shchedrin, zhizn' i tvorchestvo* (1955; previous editions 1939, 1948); Goriachkina, *Satira Saltykova-Shchedrina* (1965). For full references, see select bibliography.

50. Bushmin, *Satira Saltykova-Shchedrina* (1959) (an extract is given in

section 2); Pokusaev, *Revoliutsionnaia satira Saltykova-Shchedrina* (1963). For full references, see select bibliography.

51. Nikolaev, *M. E. Saltykov-Shchedrin, zhizn' i tvorchestvo* (1985); Prozorov, *Saltykov-Shchedrin* (1988). For full references, see select bibliography. An extract from Prozorov appears in section 2.

52. I. B. Pavlova, "Problema voploshcheniia ideala v romane Saltykova-Shchedrina *Gospoda Golovlëvy*" (The problem of the embodiment of the ideal in Saltykov-Shchedrin's *The Golovlyovs*), *Izvestiia Akademii nauk SSSR, Seriia literatury i iazyka*, 35: 13–21.

II   CRITICISM

"Blagonamerennye rechi" g. Shchedrina

A. M. SKABICHEVSKII

[Skabichevskii (1838–1910) was a critic, publicist, and regular contributor to *Notes of the Fatherland* [*NF*] during Saltykov's editorship of that journal. This extract is from a review of the first Golovlyov episode, "Family Court."]

Mr. Shchedrin's *Well-Intentioned Speeches*, in the present episode entitled "Family Court," differ considerably in content from all the customary topics that are the concern of Mr. Shchedrin's satires and that we have seen in all the preceding *Well-Intentioned Speeches*. Here we see passing before us not the pompadours, Tashkentians, wheelers and dealers, plutocrats, lawyers, and other such heroes of our contemporary life; this is not a social satire lashing those new cancers of society that have come to full flower in the present time; no, this is a story of everyday life, historical, if you like, because it depicts for us the manners of a now bygone past, which, although it became the past only yesterday, has still now entered the realm of history. Here to the fore is not that stinging salt of witty, well-targeted derision and exposé by caricature of the more absurd aspects of life, not, in short, those qualities of Mr. Shchedrin's satire to which we are accustomed; no, we have before us here a masterly sketch of types of the now bygone past, a profound, psychological analysis, and satire in the narrow sense has been replaced by a bitter humor which, by the end, is transformed into stunning tragedy of a very particular kind. In short, Mr. Shchedrin seems in this story to be a different writer. He reveals to us here new and previously untapped aspects of his talent. Some like it; others, who would like Mr. Shched-rin to continue treating only the most topical and up-to-date issues of life, find the story to be at least fifteen or twenty years behind the times and even to have an aura of archeological dust about it. As far as I am concerned, I will grant that of course Mr. Shchedrin's story deals with a subject that is not topical, and of course it would be a pity if he were suddenly to stop writing on contemporary themes and took to writing only stories such as this: in such a case, we would have gained a brand new talented writer, but we would have lost Mr. Shchedrin. Nonetheless, one such story in the sequence of all that Mr. Shchedrin has written and will write not only does no harm, but, on the contrary, may prove to be an essential link in the whole immense chain of his writings, and, although at first sight it may have a whiff of the archeological, one cannot say that it is totally lacking in vital contemporary significance. Thus everyone knows that in recent times one of the major concerns of [our] literature has been the so-called cultural manifestations of our life, that is, those things that constitute the essence of Russian life, of Russian man-ners, unadulterated by anything alien or extraneous. Mr Shchedrin's story is indisputably of the keenest interest in that it plainly presents to us these features in a few highly typical examples of them, types who are remarkable precisely because they have grown up on Rus-sian soil and in every least feature of their social behavior are the very embodiment of age-old features of Russian life free from any extra-neous admixture. On reading the story one involuntarily exclaims: Here you have real Russians, not idealized, not invented – here they are living, actual representatives of what we, by custom, call the cultivated class: we are all of us indisputably flesh of their flesh and bone of their bone.

"Vymorochnyi" N. Shchedrina

V. V. MARKOV

[Markov (1834–83) was a poet, critic, and translator. He published in various journals, including the moderate liberal *Sankt-Peterburgskie vedomosti*. The following is part of his review of "Escheated."]

In the August [1876] issue [of *NF*] Mr. Shchedrin continues his long epic of the Golovlyov family and, under the title "Escheated," depicts the going to seed of the main member of the family – the venomous Judas. We have said before that we are not among the devotees of this epic, which is written not in the accustomed manner of Shchedrin's works. The author had the wish to figure here in the role of objective artist and vested his satire in solemn attire; but to us it seems he has poorly fulfilled his purpose. Pungent wit, satiric mirth – those precious qualities of Mr. Shchedrin's talent – are here almost entirely absent, and Mr. Shchedrin has himself voluntarily abandoned the attributes of his power. The very character of Judas appears to us extremely artificial, contrived, and far removed from psychological truth. In the depiction of Judas there is absolutely no sign of the devices of objective creation that the author evidently strove to attain. There is not even any strain of humor, and the tone adopted is purely of the denunciatory-didactic order. . . . The character of Judas is drawn in such a way as only the most inveterate satirist would draw it, one who sees only the dark side of human nature. It is naked, cutting satire and nothing more, though for a true satiric impression, that refreshing, clarifying laughter which gives to a satiric portrayal higher significance is lacking. As a result, there is neither objective artistry nor vivid, truthful satire. Most important, however, there is no evidence in these stories of the creative brush – that quality of inspiration which gives true value to a literary work. Only in two places does this inspiration show through: in the comic letter of the two provincial actresses who gaily describe their carousing with lawyers, and then in the scenes where Judas, stupefied by his isolation and given over to wild, fantastic daydreaming, recalls his past, how he managed his estate, caught peasants felling his timber, and lent corn at fearsome usurers' rates. These passages are good, and one can sense in them some satirical spark. Then Judas as a character is extremely monotonous, and all his speeches are nothing but elaborations on the theme of hypocritical humility. He consists, in fact, entirely of speeches, and we see him constantly talking, chattering, and never acting; apart from this, all these speeches smack strongly of having been made up. The best feature of the stories on the Golovlyov family is their painstaking finish and conscientious composition – qualities far from always found in Mr. Shchedrin's hastily written works.

Kharakteristiki sovremennykh deiatelei: M. E. Saltykov-Shchedrin

M. [A.] PROTOPOPOV

[Protopopov (1848–1915) was a Populist critic and contributed reviews to *NF* and the radical *Delo*. The view he expresses in this extract (from a general article on Saltykov) – that the finale of *The Golovlyovs* reconciles the reader to Porfirii – has more than once been quoted by Soviet works on Saltykov for the purpose of rejecting it.]

In the artistic talent of Saltykov we find an unusually fortunate combination of elements that are rarely found together – the comic and the tragic. In the latter respect, as a psychologist and pathologist Saltykov is little known, incomparably less well know than he is as a satirist. However, a single work such as *The Golovlyovs* is quite sufficient to assure lasting fame to the writer as a remarkable analyst and major artist in the depiction of social mores. True, this is not a novel or tale but a kind of fragmented chronicle, totally devoid of plot or movement – a series of passing sketches. But these are failings only of form. For the outward absence of unity and construction there is generous recompense in the distinctness of the basic idea that runs through all these "sketches" and in the amazing consistency of the general tone, which is solemn, serious, and sad. There is not a trace of laughter, nor even of irony, but only unmixed bitterness and disconsolate sorrow for man. This "man" is not an abstraction, not some "universal man" as in Dostoevsky, but a Russian citizen of the cultivated class, our own contemporary, taking his measure of participation in our affairs. True, Saltykov's heroes are not public men in the normal sense of the word. They lead an almost exclusively personal life, but the point is that the life they lead and their whole moral personality in general are deformed not by some fortuitous conjunction of negative circumstances, but by what one might call reasons of a historical nature. There is nothing elementally evil in these people, and they are not blameworthy except for their "empty thought, empty talk, and empty hearts." Nonetheless, they poison dozens of people's lives, bring them to drink, to prostitution, to suicide . . . and all this is done in the sure conviction that their actions are right and just.

A moral suffocation seizes you when you enter this family whose abomination of desolation is starkly exposed by Saltykov. What is going on here: whether it is obtuseness or inhumanity that causes all these "killings" – is difficult to make out. We are confronted with people who live in human society, in our society, but who are totally detached from any human purpose. They are miserly, reckon every last farthing, keep a tally of "morsels" – only ask them for whom and why they do it. They are religious and constantly invoke the name of God, but they take the name of God in vain and their religion is repulsive humbug. Religious feeling as the aspiration to an ideal, as the inculcation of moral principles, as the light of love, is absolutely unknown to them; all they know is ritual and the dead formality of dogma. They play the hypocrite and deceive no one. They have everything and in fact need nothing, for they lack what is most important: a meaning of life, a purpose for existence. Their life is an endless rigmarole, a state of vegetation that is burdensome to others, savorless and tasteless to themselves. They have no feelings, only habits. They are not even egoists, for egoism sets a program, however false, while they know nothing but routine and stagnation. They love no one, perhaps because no one has loved them . . . , but most likely because love imposes obligations, and to love a person means entering into that person's life, being concerned for his or her happiness, and also inevitably placing restrictions on one's own personality, and this is inconvenient, trying, troublesome, and often financially disadvantageous. At the same time they are complacent and take refuge in their opinionatedness like a snail in its shell, and no proofs, no lessons of life have the power to shift them from their view. They are model Christians, because they never miss a service and punctiliously hold commemoration services for their children who have perished from cold and hunger; they are model citizens because they commit no acts that are punishable by written law and outdo any village constable in their political soundness; they are, finally, highly moral people, because they live "by a strict moral code." Their conscience is clear and their peace of mind is undisturbed, as undisturbed as the green water of a stagnant pond. If they perform vile deeds, they do so invariably under the cover of authority or the law ("It's not what I wish, but what the law commands") or of God himself . . . . [Protopopov here points out that such people as Arina Petrovna and Porfirii Golovlyov are convinced of their own rightness and are upheld in this conviction by the opinion of their milieu: Arina Petrovna, for instance, is admired for her prudent estate management and acquisitions of property, with no regard taken of the means by which she operates.]

In the person of Judas . . . "empty thought" and "empty-heartedness" found even sharper expression than in his mother. Judas is not only an acquisitor, he is a moralist to boot; he is the theorist and philosopher of that code of living to which his milieu subscribes. Even the "increases" and "roundings off" of his property he carries out not from greed, but rather, it would seem, on principle, from a sense of civic duty. What can a peasant's overdue three-roubles debt mean to him? Nonetheless, he claims it with an astonishing persistence, brings the court into action, writes requests, all manner of petitions and appeals, and knows no peace until "justice," as he understands it, is triumphant, that is, until he can note in the appropriate column of his ledger "3 roubles, borrowed by such and such, repaid such and such date." Judas is a fanatic for form, to which he will sacrifice any kind of substance, even the most basic human feelings. . . . He is not afraid to send his mother packing on grounds of law (no other way). . . . In the name of the same formal morality he brought one of his sons to suicide and the other to Siberia. . . .

[Protopopov quotes the interview in which Porfirii rejects Petia's plea for help.]

Be indignant, rage, castigate, if you wish. But remember that to do so is useless and unjust – I repeat, *unjust*. We have witnessed a crime but see no criminal. Judas's actions are conscious and, moreover, systematic; that I will not only acknowledge but emphasize. Yet still we are not faced by a criminal in the dock. A criminal is someone who tramples on the moral law; can we really accuse Judas of having done that? Judas observes *his own* moral rules in such a way as to provide a model of consistency and implacable firmness, and if in practice these rules lead [him] to something close to "child killing," the fault lies not with him but with the "rules" themselves, with the morality he has assimilated. "You got yourself into this mess, then get yourself out"; "You like to ride on a sledge, then like pulling one, too" – in what way are these not principles? We can revolt against their inward meaning, dispute and decry the ideas they embody, but we cannot deny the regulatory function they have for a certain class of people, because this function is a fact. I will go further and unhesitatingly call Judas, the killer of his son, a hero. What did he in fact do? He sacrificed his son on the altar of his morality. Can there be any greater heroism, can the triumph of an idea, a conviction be given more decisive expression? That Judas was governed by conviction . . . is beyond doubt. The author presents him neither as Harpagon [the miser in Molière's play *L'Avare* – ED.], nor as a cannibal with a love for cannibalism. It was not the wretched three thousand [roubles] by which he might have saved his son that mattered to Judas; he cared about the principle – a revolting, short-sighted, inhuman, senseless principle, in which, though, he believed and by which alone he lived. . . .

Judas is a man of principle. His cold-blooded cruelty, his wooden lack of feeling stem not from his purely personal qualities – meanness, egoism, and so on – but chiefly from the fact that he has an armory of theoretical "maxims" that sanction his conduct. In Judas, Saltykov presents to us the ultimate, the most complete representative of commonplace morality, a morality which through [his portrayal of] him he condemns and scorns. In this is contained the whole significance of the novel, a vast significance, since in place of [this] outlived ideal he puts forward a new, more humane ideal. A change of this sort in the guiding moral ideals in the life of an individual or equally in the life of a society brings on crises that lead to renewal and salvation. . . .

Saltykov ends his story as a moralist with the triumph of a higher moral truth. He rehabilitates Judas in our eyes, he makes him lament, with the bitter tears of a late repentance, the senseless, inhuman life he has led. The better qualities of human nature, so long suppressed [in him] by the dead hand of traditional morality, finally gain the ascendancy – too late to make him a new man but still in time to make him expiate by suffering all the evil he has done. . . .

In terms of artistry and psychology, Judas's moral enlightenment is extremely well motivated. The shattering episode of Liubin'ka and Annin'ka, an episode which, for tragic power of presentation, little in our literature can equal, is, for the reader, a psychological stimulus sufficient to affect even Judas. And yet . . . is there not here some strain on the truth of life, more specifically on the truth of *prosaic* life, the truth of ordinary gray reality? Alas! In this real life the Judases retain confidence in their rightness till their last gasp, are not tormented by pangs [of conscience], do not see phantoms at their bedside, and die "unashamed and peaceful" in expectation of their entry into the bosom of Abraham. It would be an easy matter to live in the world if crime contained within itself its own retribution, but real life offers us different impressions and different results. . . .

Russkii roman i russkoe obshchestvo

K. GOLOVIN

[Golovin (1843–1914) was a liberal critic and prose writer. This extract is from his study entitled *The Russian Novel and Russian Society*.]

A tragic note has generally been present in Shchedrin's talent.

This he brilliantly demonstrated in his epic of the Golovlyov family. In this most substantial – both by size and content – of his literary works Saltykov, with truly Shakespearian power, revealed to what monstrous lengths moral evil in man, nourished by two such impulses as hypocrisy and cupidity, can go. The figure of Judas is a living example of how a hidden passion gradually consumes not only the spiritual but also the physical organism, destroying a man by the very attainment of that for which he strives. The avidity of Judas gradually increases in its abominable power, grows ever more petty in its outward manifestations, destroys in him not only all human feeling, but the very content of his own life. In this, his only large-scale work, Saltykov, more than anywhere else, reveals himself as a profound psychologist.

True, *The Golovlyovs* is not free of a major defect: it is extremely long-winded, and this makes it tiresome reading. But the impression it creates remains nonetheless powerful for the fact that Saltykov ministered punishment to his repulsive hero not through any conflict with his milieu, but by means of an inner judgment, a conscious realization of the total void within him. Judas triumphed over everyone and, as one by one he lost the unloved members of his immediate circle, he experienced neither sorrow nor repentance. But when the last of these intimates disappeared, he suddenly realized that he himself had caused the desolation of his life, and the burden of isolation crushed him.

In our critical literature the attempt has often been made to find in *The Golovlyovs* a stern denunciation of serfdom and the dissolution of the gentry. But to understand Saltykov's novel in this sense is to enlarge its significance in one aspect and to reduce it too much in another. Judas is not the representative of a class; as a type, he is completely individual and at the same time universal. He is terrible not as a slave owner, and his pitiless greed, thinly concealed beneath the mask of submissive hypocrisy, is not a product of the easy life of the gentry; rather, it is a spiritual cancer that could infect a man of any circle. There are Judases not only in Russia and not only in the gentry class.

In the novels of Balzac and Dickens one can find several characters who are very close to Saltykov's hero. In *The Golovlyovs* not only is it impossible to perceive any scenes specifically related to the institution of serfdom; on the contrary, Judas is rather a product of [our] more recent times. In comparison with him, his mother, once the autocratic wealthy landowner, is almost sympathetic, and the heartless oppression that is suffered in turn by those close to Judas falls harder on his family than on his serfs. We should note, incidentally, that the custom of regarding Shchedrin as primarily a denouncer of serfdom and a direct supporter of the radicalism of the 1860s is founded on a patent misunderstanding. Shchedrin of course had a deep hatred of the pre-reform ways, and this hatred was shared with him by all or practically all of his contemporaries. But his main target was scarcely the class from which he himself had come. Only once – in the last of his works, *Old Times in Poshekhon'e* – did he present a graphic and somewhat one-sided picture of the infamy of landowners; but even this picture pales when set against the countless sketches he wrote about social and public life – not, moreover, social and public life before the reforms but, for the most part, that which was contemporary with the movement of the 1860s and 1870s. Apart from ignorance and violence – those old survivals from pre-reform times, Shchedrin hated above all the complacent lie that turned even the best reforms into a fresh source of evil; a lie, moreover, that lay not only in people but in what might be called the unconscious process of life itself. Shchedrin's outlook on life caused him to see a target in everything, because he expected from life nothing but evil, because he regarded life as ground where only tares can grow. In the very nature of things he sensed some deep and malicious irony, being more distrustful of attempts to cure society than he was of its old ills.

Literaturnye kharakteristiki

A. I. VVEDENSKII

[Vvedenskii (1844–1909) contributed critical articles and reviews to many journals. His articles on Saltykov, reprinted in his *Literaturnye kharakteristiki* (Literary characterizations), date from the 1880s.]

The author points to three characteristics that run through the history of the family: "idleness, incapacity for activity of any kind, and hard drinking." The first two brought with them empty talk and empty thought; the hard drinking was only, as it were, simply the necessary conclusion to "the general shambles of life." It is evident that all these features merge in one, and that is "idleness"; the rest are its consequences. Idleness, idleness, and idleness – that is the essential content of this life.

All these general characteristics are given to us by the author. Let us now look at what is said by the characters he presents and what their life is. In all seven stories that make up the work, two figures principally stand out and rise to their full height before the reader: the mistress Arina Petrovna and her favorite son Porfirii Vladimirych – Judas. In the family drama of decline and dissolution it is they who play the principal and active part. Around them is grouped a series of secondary characters whose fate is extremely tragic. They are not evil; on the contrary they are very nice, good people, endowed with fine qualities; they possess brains and a very human heart. But what becomes of them all! Here we have Stepan Golovlyov, the eldest brother of Judas and unloved son of Arina Petrovna. With what sort of upbringing did fate provide him? His mother, the author tells us, was "altogether too independent, too much of a 'bachelor' to see anything in her children but a superfluous burden." The outcast "Scallywag Stëpka," a clever boy, had from childhood fulfilled the role of part pariah, part jester, and he became "Booby Stëpka." Constant humiliation combined with idleness naturally makes an impressionable boy servile, forms him into a person lacking in independence, easily subject to any influence, and, besides that, inactive. He is one of those talented natures of which the author gives examples in *Provincial Sketches*. He completed the *gymnasium* course, entered a university, but since in school and in life he only encounters a repetition of his family, he sinks lower and lower. The disfavor of his mother, who provided him with few means, develops in him inclinations and capacities that fit him not for independent life and activity, but for the role of hanger-on. How familiar this is to anyone who has observed at close hand the life of our society. What is there to say of the results of such a preparation for life? They are only too obvious. The first collision with life and Stepan Golovlyov must come to ruin. And of course that is just what happened; the author gives an excellent description of how, step by step, this man perishes physically, mentally, and morally, how gradually his head and his heart are worn away. Reader, recall one of the famed heroes of our fiction, Oblomov. Stepan Golovlyov is Oblomov exactly, only less advantageously placed in life. If the respected Il'ia Il'ich [Oblomov] had not had such a loving mother and had had, moreover, a brother like Judas, he would have found himself drawing a line under life long before that apartment in the Petersburg quarter with the flashing elbows of his housekeeper, the government clerk's widow.

One need not speak of Judas's father, nor of his other brother Pavel, nor of his nieces; they are all Booby Stëpkas with only the slightest of variations in character and, mainly, in their life situations. Pavel Golovlyov ends in exactly the same way as Stepan; he only holds out longer because he is less unloved by "dear Mother." But his whole life passes under the same influences. Naturally they all, and later Judas's nieces too, flee from their native, but "dead" home; life takes them into its cold embraces and finally breaks them. We say this about life on purpose. Just consider the people our heroes encounter outside their "dead home." They are all Booby Stëpkas like themselves, or Judases along with "dear Mother." Not one of our heroes meets with support or sympathy or any moral influence; all around is darkness with no prospect of light. There is no way out for them except either to return home to where generation after generation has awaited dispatch to slaughter [*umertvie*] or to make their way into the camp of "the triumphant, staining their hands red with blood," but here, too, their path is blocked by their rivals, representatives of the "successful" families who, as the author puts it, "blandish first and then betray," examples of which we see in other works by the author. But for this home to which they can return, fate would perhaps lead them on to that road called the "Vladimirka" [the road to Vladimir, the first stage of the route taken by convict-convoys on their way to Siberia – ED.].

Judas and "dear Mother" are the active members of the family. They are both landowners-acquisitors. They have known how to pursue their ends and have actively managed their affairs, but what do they come to: only to an awareness of the needlessness of their activity, to a void. By his own example Judas showed his mother what she had been to others, and she died in the awareness of the odium contained in her lifetime's activity. Judas is finally brought to the same conclusion and to the realization that it is too late, that life should have been something quite different from what he had reckoned it to be; he realizes all his callousness, remembers his victims, but only too late. With great artistic perspecuity the author marks the main moments in the psychological life of his heroes, their gradual shifts to consciousness of the destructive quality of their lives. How did this failed life of theirs come about? In Judas, his mother's favorite, we can see her influence, the influence of her acquisitive activity and of that age-old morality, whose influence we also see in Chichikov. Reader, recall the injunctions that the hero of [Gogol's] *Dead Souls* heard repeated and that entered into his soul – be obedient to your seniors, and so on. Judas went into life with just such a stock of practical moral maxims, which in him found expression in what the author calls empty talk and empty thought. Judas's fate was clearly inevitable in just the way the author describes to us. Left in isolation and seeing nothing but hatred around him, in the end he must come to that oppressive awareness that inflicts his punishment on him.

The characters in Mr. Saltykov's work are clearly old acquaintances of ours, only seen in a new light and in new circumstances. From the same family the author brings forth both the Oblomovs and the Chichikovs, only they are less successful – the genuine ones must be sought in the "successful" families. This, in our view, reflects a profound understanding of our life. These two prime types indeed represent only the consequences of the same influences of life on different natures, or even on identical natures in different situations. The reader might ask: what are these influences? You have only to look around and all will be clear. You see a society in turmoil, striving to find some way out of its age-long helplessness. Everything in it is divided because all individuals have to fend for themselves and know not whether in others they should see a friend or foe. You hear in it no living word. Picture to yourself in the midst of this chaos a man of good heart who knows no way out and anyway is accustomed to a carefree existence at the expense of others. Where can such a man go? . . . But what a broad field is open to the Chichikovs! . . . The time will come when the tasks of every individual will become clarified; education will gain strength; the feeble will, albeit slothfully, take up some activity – it will otherwise be impossible to exist; the strong will become their leaders; society will be more active; and our descendants will no longer experience the sad fate of their ancestors who have been corrupted by their age-long existence on the labor of the people.

Satira Saltykova-Shchedrina

A. S. BUSHMIN

Scarcely any other character in Shchedrin has been the subject of such searching analysis as Judas. However, one aspect of this type has so far not been fully elucidated. Judas is regarded almost exclusively as a symbol of the moral and social collapse of the serf-owning class. This significance of the character is indeed fundamental. Judas Golovlyov personifies the landowning class at the time of its historically determined fall. A life founded on parasitism, acquisitiveness, and tyranny brings its own inevitable "retribution." People become dehumanized: they degenerate morally and physically.

Arina Petrovna, her children, and her grandchildren – these three generations, who depart with ever increasing rapidity from the land of the living – reflect three consecutive stages in the history of the decline of the landowning class. The world of the Golovlyovs is one inhabited by reptiles who devour one another. But it is to be noted that the most reptilian of the reptiles in the Golovlyov world – Judas – is the most tenacious of life. So full of vitality was this member of the second generation of the dying breed that, before coming to his own shameful end, he had driven to the grave all who became in the least way entangled in his web, including his sons and nieces. Judas, longer than any other, succeeded in coming off unscathed. His moral insensitivity, his total, stubborn, bestial indifference to others, his "well-intentioned" mendacity were for him a sure shield.

In developing with relentless consistency the theme of the destruction of a parasitic personality, Shchedrin, in *The Golovlyovs*, is thus far from the idea that even such corrupt and empty-hearted types as Judas will die out of their own accord and that it can be left to history to perform its own cleansing process. In dying, Judas pours forth a deadly poison. His pre-death convulsions are a danger to those about him. His path to the grave is strewn with the corpses of his many victims. The Judas type, as he steps over the corpses, is infected by the stench of their decay but still continues on his murderous way until the very moment of his final moral and physical collapse. It is for this reason that the perfectly reasonable view that Shchedrin, in Judas Golovlyov, demonstrated the inevitable downfall of such types, requires substantial amplification and more precise definition.

[Shchedrin] once stated that the death of the hero in a fictional work is [merely] a one-off death and that in real life the hero remains alive for as long as the corresponding order of things is maintained. This is true also of Judas Golovlyov. In Shchedrin's work he died a shameful death. For a section of the landowning-gentry class this was already an accomplished fact. In "Dvorianskaia khandra" and *Ubezhishche Monrepo* [For more on *Ubezhishche Monrepo* (The Refuge of Mon Repos), see the introduction, pp. 25–26; "Dvorianskaia khandra" (Gentry depression), an 1878 sketch, has a similar theme. – ED.] Shchedrin portrayed the "unashamed" process of dying of cultivated, liberally inclined landowners. This also was a reflection of real-life facts. But in respect to the landowning class as a whole, these "shameful" and "unashamed" deaths depicted by Shchedrin were one-off examples. The satirist pronounced a death sentence on the landowning class, historically doomed and already dying out, but still flourishing politically and asserting its claim to class supremacy. In real life, the serf-owning Judases, [though] condemned by history, continued to exist for as long as the monarchic "order of things" that supported them remained in place.

The Golovlyovs shows not only how representatives of a historically doomed class die off but also how they exert themselves to lengthen their existence. Judas symbolizes the historical doom of the exploiters belonging to the age of feudal serfdom and, at the same time, represents their crafty, predatory resourcefulness. Thanks to their resourcefulness, their mendacity, and their zoological callousness, they go on living considerably longer than the span allotted to them by history. "In general," Shchedrin says of Judas, "he was a man who avoided disturbance of any kind and who was sunk to the ears in a morass of trivialities relating to his own shabby self-preservation" (*SS*, 13:140).

Judas's jesuitical prattle and treacherous ways are not only a symptom of the decay of a class that has outlived its time but also an indication of the desperate efforts and treacherous ploys to which the parasitic dregs of humanity resort in order to save their skins, lengthen their existence, and hold on to their tottering supremacy in society.

Thus the figure of Judas personifies the most repulsive as well as the most resilient species of the parasitic class of feudal, property-owning exploiters at a time when their dominion was collapsing. In considering the import of the figure of Judas Golovlyov, we should therefore distinguish his narrow and his broad historical significance. If the first consists in the fact that he, as a social type of the Russian gentry, embodies the essence of feudal parasitism, the second lies in the fact that, as a psychological type, he personifies the essence of every kind of hypocrisy and treachery and, as such, passes beyond the context of any one historical period, any one class, any one nation.

Judas Golovlyov's sphere of activity is the manorial estate. Here, like a spider, he has spun his web and awaits his victims. He is wholly imbued with the traditions of feudal rapacity and pre-reform pettifogging bureaucracy, of which he has had thirty years of experience. The manorial estate is the cradle of Judas and the first arena for his actions. However, the Judas type is entirely conceivable in other spheres of activity and at other stages of development of the exploitative society. As a social type, Judas represents a class departing from the historical scene; as a psychological type, he goes far beyond the social milieu that formed him. The psychology of a class survives considerably longer than the class that framed it. When a class departs from the historical scene, its psychology long continues to exist in survivals of the past and retains its significance in the conservative tradition. And if, in the social-economic structure of Russia, the remains of serfdom continued to exist right up to the revolution, they persisted still more durably in the psyche and ideology of certain strata in the ruling classes. Because of this, the Judas type created by Shchedrin remains significant not only historically but also actually.

That is not all. As a psychological type, Judas relates not only to the feudal past. He contains features that were common to both moribund serfdom and the capitalist order that was to replace it. It is not incidental that Judas, entirely a product of the world of feudal barbarity, is shown in the novel principally as a person operating in post-reform circumstances.

Hypocrisy of every kind, used as a means to deceive the popular masses, is an inseparable feature of the morality of all ruling, exploiting classes in general. Hypocrisy is inherent in the bourgeoisie to an even greater degree than in the gentry. The dominion of the gentry landowner was founded on the legal right to own land and serfs. The dominion of the bourgeois entrepreneur is founded on the economic exploitation of "free labor" in conditions of – legally abolished – slavery. Consequently, the bourgeoisie is forced all the more often to have recourse to hypocrisy as a curb to keep the oppressed masses in obedience. It was not by chance that Shchedrin chose the title *Well-Intentioned Speeches* for his work describing the start of the triumphant march of the Russian bourgeoisie in the first post-reform decade. Well-intentioned speeches are, above all, those hypocritical speeches of the bourgeoisie about the common good, the sacred law of property, the interests of society and the state, all of which were summoned up to mask the triumph of capitalist cash, to ennoble the selfish pursuit of capital. The lying of the prayerfully pious litigant, usurer, and hypocrite, Judas Golovlyov, fits exactly into this chorus of well-intentioned speeches. It is not for nothing that he figures in the cycle so entitled. In his hypocrisy Judas is boring, patriarchal, barbarously uncouth, and sickeningly banal: he acts the hypocrite in his patrimonial estate, in the family circle, at the domestic dinner table. But in its essence, in its predatory purpose, Judas's lying is no different from the more skilled, more new-fashioned lying of the bourgeois man of affairs. Judas is second to him not in mendacity but only in the art of lying. Psychologically Judas represents a type in whom the ways of serfdom intersect with those of the bourgeoisie, and in whom is achieved, one could say, the moral fraternity of two exploiting classes – the declining gentry and the rising bourgeoisie. Consequently, the unmasking of the hypocrisy of Porfirii Golovlyov the serf-owner has, objectively, the significance of a condemnation of the morality of property-owning exploiters in general, of the morality of predators of various shapes and various spheres of activity.

Roman M. E. Saltykova-Shchedrina "Gospoda Golovlyovy"

K. N. GRIGOR'IAN

[Grigor'ian discusses the ending of the novel and cites the statement of E. I. Pokusaev that in "The Reckoning" the "acquisitive landowner and prattler" (Judas) comes to be "perceived in a truly tragic light."]

The question naturally arises: What prompted such an ending? If the author sees in his hero only the landowner and prattler, the acquisitive "bloodsucker" for whom he has nothing but scorn and hatred, then what need was there for [these] tragic features in the description of the last stage of Judas's life? In the opinion of E. I. Pokusaev, the source of this tragic element lies in the author's desire to make Judas realize the full squalor of his fall and the impossibility of escape from his situation. "The revelation of a tragic element of this kind," E. I. Pokusaev writes, "intensifies the criticism, intensifies the denunciation of a social order that deforms the human personality and reduces it to the situation of Judas."

Saltykov's social standpoint could not fail of course to have some influence in determining his hero's fate. But this alone does not explain the tragic tones in the concluding part of *The Golovlyovs*. The author was undoubtedly also moved by the psychological problem. Judas not only represents a class, he is also a psychological type.

Judas is depicted by Saltykov as a representative of a degenerating, dying class. In his psychological characterization his class parameters are clearly marked and the historical ground shown on which this monstrous figure arises. He is "a middling landowner," an acquisitor, a predator, a "bloodsucker," who "in peace and harmony," "gently, gently, bit by bit," "making no haste, praying God's good grace" oppresses, harries, tortures, and dispossesses all around him, starting with the peasants and ending with members of his own family. It is impossible to view Judas outside specific historical reality, outside the milieu that bred him, outside the general atmosphere of the age of serfdom. The point is, though, that in his artistic treatment of the hypocrite-prattler type, Saltykov attained such perfection and in his creation achieved such depth of psychological truth, such power of generalization, that it would be erroneous to confine the significance of Judas to his membership in a social class or to a particular historical context. Such a view would considerably impoverish the substance of the figure, would reduce the "objective greatness" (Goncharov) of Judas as a social-psychological type.

. . . Judas is a complex psychological type. He is endowed not only with features that characterize him as a landowner, predator, and representative of the degenerating gentry; he is at the same the bearer of universal human vices. Problems of morality were by no means alien to the author of *The Golovlyovs*, and the psychological exposure of hypocrisy was a task of not the least importance in his creative consciousness.

Saltykov's course was to present with growing depth one particular psychological trait, by a multilayered revelation, in a variety of situations. Each concrete incident or episode opens up some new aspect, some new particulars of Judas's hypocritical nature. Saltykov avoided being schematic, painting a mask of moral deformity. His interest was in the task of creating a psychological portrait of the hypocrite.

It was for this reason that out of the many possible variants for the ending of the novel he chose the one that was most complicated and difficult in just this psychological respect. Saltykov showed how in the repugnant person of Judas, sunk in baseness and vileness, in the extremes of moral degradation, there awakes something "human," something like the pangs of conscience.

The author makes Judas, as his life is ending, look into his desolate soul and shudder. In this, though, there is of course no possible question of sympathy or pity for the "bloodsucker." The author's position remains unchanged: the unending sequence of Judas's crimes, his predatory ways, his callousness and cruelty, his sophisticated devices for oppression, his cynicism and hypocrisy – all this evokes in the author . . . a natural feeling of disgust and indignation. He shows Judas as the hypocrite and "bloodsucker" he detests, who spent his life in tormenting, tyrannizing, torturing his own and others, without sparing anyone who crossed his path. Yet despite this, there is at the end of the novel a tragic resonance. The final pages of *The Golovlyovs* are written in such a way as to leave no doubt that there arose in Judas something like pangs of conscience. . . . His decision to seek forgiveness at his mother's grave was taken after long and painful deliberation. The behavior of Judas changes sharply. At the end of his life's journey he appears to be transformed, different, he shows signs of suffering.

The author could have rounded off the novel with the natural death of his hero. But such a resolution did not satisfy Saltykov. He had to devise for Judas some more terrible end. A sense of justice demanded that before departing from life Judas should himself experience the moral torment and torture that he caused to others so that he might in some measure realize his own guilt, the monstrosity of the crimes he has committed, and all the uselessness, senselessness, and somber desolation of his miserable existence. Even on the last pages of the novel Saltykov is merciless to the hypocrite and "bloodsucker." Judas's "neglected conscience" awoke only when he was on the verge of death, when he was weak and feeble and could no longer commit new crimes. He reminds us of the murderous killer in Saltykov's fable "The Poor Wolf," who devastated the forest and "raged rampant" until old age came upon him. Then death became a blessing for him, a deliverer from his moral torments, and for death he calls. "Judas Golovlyov," writes M. S. Goriachkina, "like the betrayer in the Gospel, is cursed forever and must seek his own death. The awakened conscience, therefore, does not bring him rebirth but administers the final blow."

Saltykov-Shchedrin

V. V. PROZOROV

The finale of *Gospoda Golovlyovy* might indeed seem sudden, even almost improbable. A careful reading should restrain one from adopting an elementary, overtly sociological interpretation of the novel's ending: the evildoing landowner has got his deserts, life has sternly settled his account – and it serves the villain right! With such a simplified, summary answer, something fundamental to the author's conception will elude the reader. Its particular logic will elude him, and a complex psychological figure will be turned into an unsubtle illustration of the proposition that the collapse of the landowning class is inevitable.

Meanwhile we sense an enigmatic quality in the ending that does not yield to superficial resolutions, and we realize that this feeling stems from the whole logic of the character Saltykov-Shchedrin has created. E. I. Pokusaev has justly observed that in the ending the author "attributes to the hero such features, makes him utter such weighty, not empty, words, discovers in his fetid, failing life such actions that the sharply defined type of the acquisitive landowner and prattler is perceived in a truly tragic light."

Is it possible to speak of tragedy in respect to a nauseating liar, a man who has lived without conscience or decency? This question causes us to consider the nature of the author's attitude to the Golovlyovs and to Porfirii Vladimirych himself. Judas is, after all, the last of the line, a man who is finished. The drunkenness of empty thought has turned already into the real drunkenness of drink. Beyond that, when "all accounts with life are closed," complete physical destruction should follow. But what feelings does Porfirii Golovlyov evoke in us in the closing pages of the novel? Are there objective signs indicative of changes in the author's tone?

The nearer the dénouement, the more rarely does the author refer to Porfirii as Judas. The unctuously affectionate phrases and words almost entirely disappear from his speech. Porfirii Vladimirych talks quite differently now than before. In his words "Poor girl! My poor girl!" there is a genuine, kind of astonished pity for Annin'ka, a suddenly awakened sympathy for a fellow being. Porfirii Vladimirych does not launch into his previous verbal rigmarole. Profoundly stirred, he puts to Annin'ka one after another the fragmentary questions that torment him. The author's scorn, mockery, and irony vanish.

What force is it that brings Judas to awareness? How does the author himself explain the transformation that takes place in his hero? A terrible truth has been revealed to Porfirii Vladimirych. The "drunken conversations" with Annin'ka, her mercilessly persistent taunts, the nightmare visions that pursued the master of Golovlyovo in his half-empty house, "the constant reminders of the old deaths were bound in the end to have their effect. The natural result of this was a condition that was either fright or the stirring of conscience, and in fact the latter rather than the former."

The theme of isolation, which is linked with the principal character of the novel, does not arise suddenly, but gradually, as the last representatives of the Golovlyov stock depart from life. At first it is the isolation of Arina Petrovna still in her prime in a house full of people, isolation in the midst of her children ("For whom?"). After Arina Petrovna's death the author foretells a hard end for his hero: "He did not understand that the grave which had opened now before his eyes was bearing away his last link with the living world, the last living being with whom he could share the dust that filled his being. And that henceforth this dust, finding no release, would accumulate within him until finally it choked him."

And then (in the chapter "Illicit Family Joys") Judas himself "for the first time in his life . . . seriously and sincerely bemoaned his isolation, for the first time in his life he had some inkling that the people around him were not simply pawns to be exploited by him." When real life, fretful and unpredictable, occasionally intrudes into

Judas's existence, he is at a loss, does not know what to do, what to undertake. Nor does the death of his son Volodia pass without leaving its mark on Judas: "Occasionally there rose even in him a dim voice, which murmured that to resolve a family quarrel by suicide was suspect, to say the least" (in the chapter "Family Scores").

The master of Golovlyovo himself, torn with conscience, shattered and tormented, goes consciously to his death. His final words are addressed to Annin'ka: "You must forgive me! . . . for all . . . And for yourself . . . and for all those who are gone . . . What is it? What's happened? Where are . . . they all?"

Can it be thought that the author to some extent vindicates his hero? For Judas there is and can be no vindication. Saltykov-Shchedrin is convinced that any reconciliation with evil is immoral in the highest degree. He makes us hate his hero and at the same time not forget that evil in man does not go unpunished. Evil punishes man, and the cruelest punishment of all is the late awakening of conscience, when nothing can be changed or brought back, when the irremediable has already happened, when a man finds himself doomed to absolute spiritual isolation. Saltykov-Shchedrin reminds people of their personal responsibility for their fate. The satiric writer, whose power lay in the denunciation, the exposure of evil, gives thought to the value of human life.

It is often said that the chief guilt for a man's fall, for his empty-hearted, vile existence lies with the surrounding reality, milieu, circumstances. Saltykov-Shchedrin thought the same. However, it is also true that no reality, no milieu, no "marsh" ["Marsh" here relates to the Russian saying, used by Saltykov, "The marsh creates the demons, not the demons the marsh" – signifying that it is a corrupt system that breeds corrupt individuals, not vice versa. – ED.] removes from a man his own responsibility for himself, for his conduct in life.

In reckoning that circumstances compelled, that it was life that made a man a vile wretch and liar, there lies concealed a measure of self-justification. To say that "circumstances are to blame" is not to tell the whole truth. Can a man be absolved of guilt who in his own way, thus and not otherwise, has guided his own fate? The circumstances of life, we say, are to blame for the spiritual torpor of Judas. And what of the hero? Does he bear some measure of blame? After all, this something like "an awakening of neglected conscience," which Porfirii Vladimirych experiences with [such] terrible suddenness and power at the end of his life, is precisely a late sense of his own guilt that has suddenly stirred in him. This is the tragedy of a man who, even if unconsciously, expends to the full his spiritual stock, loses his moral props in life, and ceases to be his own master, no longer capable of changing anything in his desolate and terrible isolation.

Saltykov-Shchedrin has presented a brilliant example of a satirical work in which laughter dies on the lips, falls silent, and readers are moved to think seriously about the terrible consequences to which moral defects and moral atrophy can lead them.

Saltykov and the Russian Squire

NIKANDER STRELSKY

This book is a tragedy, not only of individuals or of a social class but of a way of life that is recurrent under externally new forms in all phases of what we call civilization. The pattern is universal and timeless. Saltykov, in his capacity as satirist, as novelist of psychological realism, has carried this pattern to its ultimate conclusion. Just as any parable is an oversimplification, an exaggeration, so is this novel. The Golovlyovs, surely, are not meant to represent all Russian landowners. They represent rather the terminal stage of a terrible moral illness to which man as a whole is subject by virtue of the very imperfections inherent in his humanness – an illness Saltykov saw as the doom of his own class in his own day. The sources of this malady were too deeply rooted, its course too far advanced, to admit the hope of evading tragedy. Redemption existed – let no one think Saltykov was a morbid fatalist – but the antidote lay only in a great spiritual regeneration, and this could occur solely by the correctives of time and suffering, by a general cultural rebirth. This hope was beyond the Golovlyovs and their kind. As individuals, as a social group, they were doomed. They had been isolated too long – isolated from one another, from the life of the spirit, from the realm of the intellect, from the larger multiple ego of the nation. To consider the non-ego, the other-than-self, gradually became an impossibility to them. They could think only of their own wants, which became ever baser; to mask this degeneration from others and from themselves they strove to make themselves ever more impervious to humanity's claim on them, while they struggled at the same time to retain their sense of living by intensifying sensation, by self-indulgence, by the empty gestures of propriety. Thus they created the coffin of their own existence. To some of them in the end this coffin was revealed; but the vision was their death blow. To rise from this whited sepulcher, to re-achieve life, required a gift of self, and the inborn capacity for such a gift they themselves had destroyed. They were all Judases, they all betrayed the divinity innate in man, and death in the case of each was, like that of Judas, a form of self-destruction.

In Saltykov's day the techniques of psychology as an analytical science were unknown, yet we can observe, as in any great creative talent, the accurate demonstration of some of its principles in his understanding of the origin and course of serfdom. In the beginning was the primal instinct for self-preservation accompanied by fear – fear, lack, want, wish, will – so far the eternal pattern was potentially normal and self-renewing. But at "will" two possibilities presented themselves: one, to dominate, to seize preservation at the cost of others; the other, to summon from one's inner resources the means to struggle, to create, to give of oneself, to cooperate with others. Serfdom meant the first alternative, the kind of domination that was essentially parasitic, psychologically an infantile regression on a grand scale. Because serfdom denied the natural dignity of man and the rights of every human being, because it refused the responsibility that is implied in the true aristocratic principle – the principle of nature, not of lineage – it was inevitably destructive, both of others and of self. It could signify in the end nothing but a form of suicide.

In these three generations of the Golovlyovs we see this process hastening to its conclusion. The first generation, Vladimir Mikhailovich and Arina Petrovna, lived to old age. The physical organism was not yet markedly impaired. Vladimir Mikhailovich was able to get himself an energetic wife and to beget nine children; for the rest, however, he created nothing, but lived on his family capital, so to speak, the viability and the worldly means his forebears had bequeathed to him. Even these things would have been lost to him, we may suppose, had not Arina Petrovna protected his existence by her vigor and enterprise. By the mercy of time he was not called upon to adjust himself to the emancipation, for which, of course, he was totally incapable.

Arina Petrovna survived as long as she did because of a kind of ruthless vigor. She had to a lively degree the ability to struggle and to create, but only in crass physical terms. Any capacity for an outgiving of self on any higher plane of being was early strangled and suppressed in her. Yet she was conscious of the lack, in a dim way. She was a lonely woman, she suffered from that loneliness, and she unconsciously revenged herself for it on all those about her. Her spiritual deterioration took on physical manifestations when the emancipation, together with encroaching senility, deprived her of all she had lived by. Her final disillusionment was like that first breath of air that strikes a long-interred coffin just unsealed, causing its contents to crumble instantly to nothingness.

The second generation retained only part of their parents' power to survive. Only four of the nine offspring reached maturity, and none exceeded middle age. Annushka's abortive effort to seize life got her a no-account husband and twin babies. Her marriage, however, was only the means she took to escape reality for the sake of self-gratification, and she could not survive the consequences. Unable to live in a positive sense, she could not even choose a suitable support for her parasitism.

Simple Simon's [i.e., Stepan's] parasitism was that of his father carried to a superlative degree of irresponsibility, a consistent death process devoid even of ruthlessness. Pavel's negative character represented something more of a blend of his parents' traits, in which their respective strong and weak features canceled each other out. His kind of passiveness permitted him a longer life span than that of Annushka or Stepan, but for all that he accomplished absolutely nothing, except perhaps that final gesture of revenge against his mother.

The third generation all perished in early youth, each in an effort to obtain something, each in a corrupt, even criminal, environment. The first generation had bequeathed to their children at least a modicum of material security in one way or another. The second generation gave nothing; indeed, it repudiated its own flesh and blood. Acute and progressive deterioration of character in the family as a whole, plus the abolition of serfdom, shut off even the turgid flow of material inheritance. True, Annin'ka and Liubin'ka had their miserable Pogorelka even at the end. The reapportionment at the emancipation would have left them, say, 150 acres, with some twenty cows and three horses. Yet so poisoned was their conception of country life, so corrupted was their own existence, that they could not even imagine taking over their own property, still less some day inheriting Iudushka's estate. Nothing remained in them of the land-owner's psychology, nothing but the age-old disease of getting with-out giving, the disease of serfdom. Everyone in this family failed completely in personal relationships. None actually earned anything in life. Whatever was obtained was gotten by some form of prostitu-tion, some betrayal of the spirit of man.

Iudushka, of course, is the concentrated expression of all this manifold failure in life. He alone inherited something of his mother's passion for accumulation; but it was a noncreative greed that evaded any effort save that involved in perpetual intrigue and the morass of meaningless details in which he submerged himself. He had no sense in practical affairs or any training as a landowner, since thirty of his mature years had been spent at a desk. When he came to Golovlyovo he brought with him only the inane and pettifogging habits of a bureaucrat, a passion for litigation and for accumulating endless scraps of paper with absurd figures that had little to do with real agriculture. His total incapacity for managing an estate would of course have ruined him in time had not his personal collapse come first. That final catastrophe was brought about, not through any external threat of church or state, but through the humble agency of Evpraksiia, who first made him aware that no man lives alone and that even he, the rich master of Golovlyovo, could not maintain the pitiful remnant of his existence without aid.

That was the first step in his final dissolution. The second was brought about by Annin'ka, who forced him to tear off the mask of hypocrisy behind which he had hidden himself from himself all his life. The shock of this revelation put an end to the long lie of his life, just as a similar revelation had done in the case of Arina Petrovna and to a lesser degree in the case of Annin'ka.

Everyone in this sordid family died meanly. In their deaths we observe an ascending climax. As the atmosphere of the book grows ever denser and more suffocating, the significance of the characters' fate becomes ever clearer to them and to the reader. In the earlier deaths we get no sense of any ultimate vision. Some dim ray of meaning, however, seems to penetrate Pavel's last hours. That meaning grows more apparent, more piercing, as one by one the others approach death, and then it finds its full expression in Iudushka's self-indictment. Yet – and here is the culminating irony – the catharsis of his soul is incomplete. Great though his agony is at the end, he cannot think of anyone but himself. In his terrible repentance it is absolution he craves – even at this moment, something for himself – and the crowning failure of his life is the failure of his death, to achieve that absolution as he faces his death. It is too late for the love of others to grow where only fear and hatred have reigned so long. Even the pang he feels for Annin'ka, the mirror of his suffering and self-accusation, is only fleeting. He is incapable of giving anything, not even his life; indeed it is taken from him, and there is no longer any person, any thing, not even his mother's grave, from which he can gain solace. Thus damned, he perishes.

One must look to the world's masterpieces to find the equals of this tragic novel. The profundity of its symbolism, its black and white simplicity, its restraint and inevitability are all marks of only the very highest talent. It has been customary to speak of Saltykov's "lack of artistry," his stylistic faults, the total absence of the poetic in him, and his unwarranted spleen; but surely only the ablest artist could so mightily conceive and so unflinchingly record such an abyss of the human spirit. The sources of the book lie, not in the exceptional, the conspicuous manifestations of life, but in the eternal drama of the commonplace, the mediocre. In portraying the doom of this obscure family of squires of nineteenth-century Russia, their delineator has given us a great parable of man's self-destruction, as searching and as true today as it was eighty years ago. As we read this book we feel about Saltykov as we occasionally feel about other authors – that he has written better than he knew, so to speak, that he has indeed overshot his own goal, and we realize that this could be true only because his creation is touched with infinity, because it springs from the innermost depths of passion, from the broadest humanity, and from the severest discipline.

Something remains to be said about the nature of Iudushka's hypocrisy. Saltykov makes it plain that it is not the hypocrisy described by Dickens or Molière, the kind that deceives society for the sake of self-interest. It is rather, he avers, a purely Russian breed, springing from another kind of society in which social principles play no part in governing behavior, one in which men "grow wild, like nettles by the fence . . . We have no need of playing the hypocrite for the sake of social principles, for we know of no such thing as social principles. We exist in perfect liberty, that is, we vegetate, lie, chatter quite naturally, without regard for principle."

Greedy as he is, Iudushka's hypocrisy is based as much on fear as on self-interest. Edmond Jaloux, in his distinguished preface to the French edition of *The Golovlyov Family*, says:

> Iudushka is afraid, and fear most often makes hypocrites, not interest. By parading their devout practices they wish to forget the vices of which they cannot rid themselves and thus to believe in a legend that may deceive God Himself. The more they sin in secret, the more they fear the Day of Judgment, and the more they increase their piety, thinking to reassure themselves. This is what Shchedrin alone has distinguished . . .
>
> Hypocrisy is a trait of character so complex, so shaded, so subtle that few writers have attempted to depict it. Furthermore, it is thought that general tolerance has tended to diminish it. Religious tolerance, perhaps, but what of political tolerance? Who will depict the comedy of the hypocritical politician, the socialist Tartuffe, of whom we have seen so many examples formed, moreover, by both fear and interest? Be assured that the

Soviet regime at this moment swarms with Iudushkas as ferocious and as quaking as this one of Shchedrin's, just as our own revolution abounded in Tartuffes and the English Reformation in Pecksniffs. As terror increases, hypocrisy increases, and it is not always before the holy ikons that hypocrisy comes to kneel in tears.

The story of the Golovlyov family is one of the most terrible accusations ever directed at any society. The figure of Iudushka, frightful in itself, becomes the more terrifying when we perceive its larger significance in terms of our own day. Yet the genius of his delineator is nowhere proven more conclusively than in the fact that he remains, not a monster, but a man, a human being who suffers even as others suffer and who evokes from us not only a sense of horror but also of pity and – yes, it is possible – even of kinship. In every man there lurks some hidden trace of a Iudushka, some ineluctable trace, that forever necessitates expiation.

The Hypocrite

V. S. PRITCHETT

We walk down a street in the dead hours of an afternoon, looking at the windows of the villas as we pass by. They are glass cases; they are the domestic aquarium, and what our idle eye is seeking, is a sight of the fish within. And presently we are taken by surprise. We see a face in one of the rooms. Agape, bemused, suspended like some torpid trout, a man or a woman is standing alone there, doing nothing, and sunk in the formidable pathos of human inertia, isolation and ennui. It is always a surprising sight and, to a novelist, a disturbing one. We are used to the actions of human beings, not to their stillness. We are taken back suddenly to our childhood, when time went by so slowly, and when we, too, were shut up in a room with some grown-up who was occupied entirely by the mysterious, enormous process of sitting. How they could sit! And sit alone! And how their figures grew larger and larger in our eyes, until their solitude and silence seemed to burst the room. It was, I think, one of the first intimations of mortality in early childhood.

The Russian novelists of the nineteenth century owe everything to their response to the man or woman sitting alone in his room, to the isolation, inertia, the off-beat in human character. They are naturally aware of what André Malraux has called in a recent book, "the crevasse that separates us from universal life." The chief subject of the Russian novelists – the monotonous life of the country house that is scores of miles from its neighbors – draws this response from them. And as they stand alone in the room, drumming their fingers on the window and looking out at the slow, cumbrous changes of cloud in the Russian sky over the steppe, the characters of the Russian novel fill out with the unoccupied hours of life. Loneliness intensifies character. The great personages of literature have so often been the solitary natures who overflow into the void that surrounds them, who transcend their personal lives and expand until they become prototypes. The Russian novel abounds in such figures. Oblomov is an example. Stepan Trofimovich in *The Possessed* is another. Iudushka of *The Golovlyov Family* belongs to this category. One is tempted to say novels are important only when they create these abnormal, comprehensive people. But in saying this it is important to note one difference between the Russian figures and those of the West. Those strong-minded, bossy, tyrannical Varvara Petrovnas and Arina Petrovnas who honk their way through Russian life like so many vehement geese; those quietly mad, stagnant, frittering men who spend their time dodging these masterful women, are different from the English eccentrics. Our eccentricity or excess is a protest against the pressure of society; the Russian excessives of the nineteenth century were the normal product of a world so lax that it exercised no pressure at all. "We Russians," Shchedrin wrote, "are not drilled, we are not trained to be champions and propagandists of this or that set of moral principles, but are simply allowed to grow as nettles grow by a fence." Iudushka and Oblomov are natural weeds of a neglected soil. They grow by running rife and they derive their force not from private fantasy alone, as Pecksniff or Micawber do, but from the Russian situation. They are puffed out by the sluggish, forgotten hours and days of the steppe. For in the empty hours and blank distances that separate them from their neighbors, all the fate, the history, the significance of Russia itself, is gazing back at their gaping eyes.

After reading Shchedrin's *The Golovlyov Family* one sees why a character like Iudushka, the liar and humbug, is greater than Pecksniff who is, I suppose, the nearest English parallel. Iudushka is greater, first, because he has Russia inside him, and, second, because he is encumbered with the dead weight of human dullness and vulgarity. He is greater because he is a bore. I do not mean that Iudushka is boring to read about. I mean that Dickens had no notion that Pecksniff was a boring and vulgar man; Dickens's mind was interested only in the dramatic and absurd exterior of the whited sepulcher. Shchedrin did not stop at the farce of human hypocrisy, for the tricks of hypocrisy are really too crude and blatant. Shchedrin went on collecting the evidence with the patience of one of those static realists like Richardson; and he presently came upon the really terrible thing in Iudushka's character. We can laugh (Shchedrin seems to say) at the obvious hypocrisies of Iudushka and, like his neighbors, we can grin at his eye-rolling, his genuflexions and his slimy whimsicalities; but there is something more serious. The real evil is the moral stagnation of Iudushka's character. The real evil is the muddle, the tangle of evasions, words, intrigues by which he instinctively seeks to dodge reality. We forgive his sins; what eludes forgiveness is the fact that his nature has gone bad, so that he himself does not know the difference between good and evil. He is a ghastly example of self-preservation at any price. In middle age he is befuddled by daydreams. He will pass a morning working out fantastic conundrums, such as how much money he would make out of milk if all the cows in the neighborhood died except his own. He works out the most detailed but essentially ridiculous systems of bookkeeping and imagines he is working. Less and less is he able to face any decision, however small. He is a hive buzzing with activity – but it is the buzz of procrastination. I do not ever remember seeing such a picture of our character in any English novel; yet the humbug's art of evading an issue by confusing it is a universal one. There is one remarkable picture of Iudushka's evasion in the account of his behavior to the servant girl whom he has got with child. Iudushka manages never to admit that the child is his, but allows everyone around to say it is. His own reaction is to groan and say, "This is unbearable" – subtly conveying that his sufferings, not his act, are what is unbearable. Iudushka reaches the sublimity of self-deception here. He has achieved detachment and isolation from his own actions. And the strange thing is that we begin to pity him at this point. He feels an agony, and we wince with him. We share with him the agony of being driven back step by step against the wall and being brought face to face with an intolerable fact.

There is nothing notably remote from our experience in *The Golovlyov Family*. Neither the emancipation of the serfs, which stupefies Arina Petrovna, nor the fact that one is reading about a remote, semifeudal estate, makes the book seem exotic or alien to us. Our own Arina Petrovnas do not starve their sons to death, but they have driven some to alcoholism; our own Iudushkas do not publicly drive their sons to suicide. But, in the main, we must be struck by the essential closeness of Shchedrin's novel to the life of the successful middle class in England. Iudushka's prayers for guidance have a sinister echo. Walter Bagehot, I believe, said that the mind of the businessman lived in a kind of twilight, and the character of Iudushka is a remarkable example of a man whose cunning requires an atmosphere of vagueness and meaningless moral maxims. He has the stupidity of the slippery. In the end, it is not so much his wickedness that shocks his nieces, as the fact that he has become such a talker, such a vulgar babbler and bore. Cucumbers, pickles, and the mercy of God indiscriminately mix in his mind. He bores one of the girls out of the house; and one of the most terrible chapters in the book is one toward the end when the girl comes back to his house to die and wonders whether she can bear to spend her last weeks in the house of a man who never stops driveling on and on about trivialities. She can tolerate him only by persecuting him. This picture of the triviality of Iudushka's mind is Shchedrin's master stroke.

The Golovlyov Family has been described as the gloomiest of the Russian novels. Certainly the characters are all wretched or unpleasant, and the reader of novels who professes that strange but common English attitude to literature – "Would I like to meet these people?" – must leave the book alone. Yet Shchedrin's book is not gloomy; it is powerful. It communicates power. It places an enormous experience in our hands. How many of the realists simply indulge in an orgy of determinism and seek only the evidence that indicates damnation. Shchedrin does this up to a point, but he is not looking for quick moral returns. His method is exhaustive and not summary. Old Arina Petrovna is a tyrant; but her lonely old age has its peculiar rewards. She enjoys guzzling with Iudushka, she adores his boring conversation; she is delighted to queer his pitch when he seduces the servant girl. The compensations of life are not moral; they are simply more life of a different kind. Here are the last years of her life:

She spent the greater part of the day dozing. She would sit down in her armchair in front of a table on which smelly cards were spread out, and doze. Then she would wake up with a start, glance at the window and without any conscious thought in her mind gaze for hours at the wide expanse of fields, stretching into the distance as far as the eye could see. Pogorelka was a sad-looking place . . . But as Arina Petrovna had lived all her life in the country, hardly ever leaving it, this poor scenery did not seem dismal to her, it touched her heart, stirring the remains of feeling that still smouldered in it. The best part of her being lived in those bare, boundless fields, and her eyes instinctively turned to them at every moment. She looked intently into the distance, gazing at the villages soaked with rain that showed like black specks on the horizon, at the white churches of the countryside, at the patches of shadow cast by the wandering clouds on the sunlit plain, at the peasant walking between the furrows, and it seemed to her that he never moved at all. But she did not think of anything or, rather, her thoughts were so disconnected that they could dwell on nothing for any length of time. She merely gazed and gazed until the drowsiness of old age began to ring in her ears, covering with a mist the fields, the churches, the villages, and the peasant walking far away.

No, Shchedrin is not gloomy because he does not soften. He undertakes to scald us with the evidence; he does not pretend that it will make vulgarity romantic or ignorance pretty. He is powerful because he remains severe. And so, at the end, when Iudushka and his niece, after their awful drunken quarrels, suddenly admit their despair to each other, and Iudushka makes the one truly heartrending cry of his life, we are moved beyond description. "Where are they all?" he cries, thinking of the mother, the brothers, the sons he has tricked and bedeviled into the very grave. He has felt the clammy coldness of a hand touching him – and the hand is his own. His cry is like Lear's. And it is all the more appalling that he utters this cry when his broken niece is still with him; if he had cried out when he was alone we would not believe it. One had indeed not grasped it until then – the total disappearance of a family, the total disappearance of all that suffering and hatred. And the force of the book is all the greater because we do not look back on a number of dramatic intrigues capped by their scenes, but we see Russia in our mind's eye, the steppe, the little-changing sky, the distance of people from one another, and the empty hours of all those lives. The English novel of family life inevitably turns from such a pessimism, but not, I think, because the English family is or was any nicer than the Golovlyovs were. The middle class, up to now, have lived in an expanding economy, which has enabled people to be independent where they could not be indulgent. If that economy becomes static or is put on the defensive, then a different tale will appear. The story of our money and of our religion has yet to be written.

M. E. Saltykov-Shchedrin:
The Golovlyov Family

I. P. FOOTE

The outstanding feature of *The Golovlyov Family* is its intensity – both in its subject matter and its style. The history of the Golovlyovs is an unrelieved catalogue of mistrust, misdeed, and wretchedness. Throughout the novel everything is dark and depressing. No opportunity for meanness is ever missed, no acts of generosity, no words of sympathy are recorded (until the final moment of Porfirii's revealed humanity when he can utter a word of pity for Annin'ka).

The setting in which Saltykov presents this history of degeneration is in keeping with the subject. As the Golovlyovs live out their lives without hope, so too is their background unrelieved by any brightness. The natural scene is uniformly dreary. The landscape is one of endless bare fields, sodden villages, black muddy roads. Skies are clouded (Stepan is oppressed in his last days by the "gray, ever weeping autumn sky"); winds are cold and penetrating. The seasons, whatever the time of year, are unfriendly. In August "the days shorten, there is a steady drizzle; the earth grows sodden; the trees stand wiltingly, dropping their yellowed leaves to the ground." October brings heavier rain, making the roads impassable and deepening the isolation of Golovlyovo. The onset of spring is no more cheerful: "Trees stood bare. There was still no sign of fresh grass even. In the distance were black fields streaked with white patches of snow." Compare the ironic "resurrection of spring" described in "The Niece" – sleet, puddles, gales, and "trees, bare of snow, swaying their sodden leafless tops in the wind." The single summer scene is as depressing. "It is noon on a hot July day. Everything seems to have died on the Dubrovino estate. . . . Even the trees stand wilting, motionless, as if exhausted. The heat seems to pour down over you in a burning wave; the earth with its covering of short burnt grass is scorching hot; everything is suffused with unbearable light." Only once is an agreeable natural scene described – the morning in spring when Stepan returns to Golovlyovo: "It is early, soon after five. A wreath of golden morning mist hangs over the road which the sun, just rising over the horizon, barely penetrates; the grass sparkles and the air is full of the smell of firs, mushrooms, and berries." But the purpose of this description is only to provide a contrast to Stepan's gloom as he returns home to "the grave" of Golovlyovo. Stepan "noticed nothing of all this."

The domestic surroundings of the Golovlyovs are also depressing. The houses are dark and old. The interiors are dingy, sometimes even squalid. The atmosphere indoors is always hot and airless. In the room where Stepan spent his last days at Golovlyovo "the ceiling was black with smoke, the wallpaper cracked, in places hanging in tatters; on the windowsills was a thick layer of black tobacco ash; cushions lay about the floor which was covered with greasy mud; on the bed was a crumpled sheet, grey with dirt." The priest's house at Voplino (visited by Annin'ka when she goes to Arina Petrovna's grave) is poor and wretched – chairs with broken upholstery, un-papered walls, stained tablecloth, faded pictures, and "a pervading smell which suggested that the room had long served as a cemetery for flies and cockroaches."

The same squalor attaches to the family's material possessions. Porfirii, in the last chapter, wears a greasy dressing gown with the padding coming out. Arina Petrovna's tears fall on the greasy collar of her old cotton blouse. She plays patience with "stinking cards." The servants are aged, deformed, or unsavory. Arina Petrovna is attended by a decrepit housekeeper and a one-eyed maid; Pogorelka is guarded at night by a lame peasant. Porfirii is waited on by a drunken footman in a stained coat who reeks of "a mixture of fish and vodka." Evpraksiia yawns and scratches herself. Ulitka casually tops and tails gooseberries in the room next to the one where Pavel lies dying.

Saltykov's use of colors is typical of the Golovlyovs' cheerless world. The predominant colors are gray, black, and white. The landscapes are entirely composed of these colors: black mud, black sodden fields, black forest, the sky white or grey with clouds thickening from grey to black. Objects observed against this background stand out as black or white – distant people "like black dots," "blackened peasant huts," the house at Pogorelka "all black from age and weather," the white bell tower of Golovlyovo, the white chapels of village cemeteries. Gray occurs especially in figurative contexts – Arina Petrovna's "gray past," "the yawning gray abyss of time," and the "gray phantoms" of dead Golovlyovs. Porfirii is a study in black and white – his clothes are black, his face pale. White is the color of death – old Vladimir Mikhailovich lying on his bed "covered with a white blanket. He wore a nightcap and was all white, like a corpse"; Pavel on his deathbed "lay on his back with a white blanket over him." Positive colors are rare, and even when they occur it is normally in a negative context: *green* [italics here and henceforth are mine. – I.P.F.] blinds keep out the light from Pavel's death chamber, Porfirii turns *green* with malice, his nose turns *red* from his emotional praying, Stepan is brought back from flight with his face *blue* and swollen. In natural descriptions such colors figure hardly at all – the trees in August drop their *yellowed* leaves. When a definite color is mentioned it is likely to be pale and faded – "the manor house once painted gray but now *faded white*," "two chests (in the priest's house at Voplino) covered with gray *faded* cloth." Even the eyes of the priest are referred to as "*once* blue."

The range of colors Saltykov uses reflects the drabness of Golovlyovo life and the family's state of decay. The same somber effect is achieved by Saltykov's setting so much of the novel in half-light or darkness. Interiors are invariably dim. Pavel dies in the half-light of his curtained room watching the flickering shadows thrown by the faint light of the icon lamp. Arina Petrovna, too, lies dying in semidarkness, blinds drawn, a flickering light cast by guttering icon lamps. The onset of evening is a favorite time of day for Saltykov. A memorable passage in the opening chapter describes Stepan gazing all day at the sky from his window until evening sets in and the visible landmarks are gradually swallowed up by the dusk.

Darkness and dusk have a figurative significance for the Golovlyovs. "Dusk" (*sumerki*) is used to describe Porfirii's moral state, and Arina Petrovna in her decline falls into a state of mental "dusk." Annin'ka's aberrations in her career as a provincial actress are categorized as "darkness" (*mrak*). As a child she had associated Golovlyovo with darkness from which she sought to escape to a "light" outside. In another context darkness is a solace to the Golovlyovs. It enables them to shut out the painful realities of life. Stepan, when evening comes, shuns the candlelight of the office and retires to his room to be alone with the darkness. He welcomes the darkness because it gives his fantasies greater scope to take him away from the reality of Golovlyovo. Annin'ka welcomes the early darkness of December and rarely lights the candles because "in the midst of this darkness she feels easier."

The lifelessness suggested by the lack of light is suggested, too, by the stillness that pervades the houses of the Golovlyovs. Shut up in their isolated apartments, usually alone, the Golovlyovs are separated from the noise and movement of life. Their element is evening and night and the "deathly silence" that reigns in the house after the day's activities have ended. Even these daily activities are remote from the Golovlyovs – they hear them as vague distant sounds that have no relevance to them. The contrast between the stillness of their rooms and the distant bustle of the house emphasizes the contrast between their moribundity and the life going on around them. The silence is oppressive and sinister. It is especially associated with Porfirii who moves noiselessly about the house on tiptoe, eavesdropping, appearing suddenly in unexpected places. The stillness, like the darkness, has symbolic overtones. In the last episode Porfirii looks from his window on the empty yard. The stillness of the yard (which would normally be a scene of activity) symbolizes not only the running down of the estate and Porfirii's lack of control, but also the turning away of life from the last master of Golovlyovo.

An important contribution to the novel's effectiveness is the intensity of Saltykov's style. Saltykov was a "strong" writer who, as a satirist and publicist, was accustomed to expressing his attitudes forcefully. In the novel, as in his satirical works, he concentrates severely on the matter at hand. Everything in *The Golovlyov Family* is related to the theme of the Golovlyovs' decay. Events and externals serve only to illuminate the family's moral and mental states. There is, for instance, barely any description of the characters' outward appearance. Of the Golovlyovs only Stepan is described at any length – in the scene depicting his return to Golovlyovo – but here we see that although reference is made to his features and dress the emphasis is on their *condition*, which reflects his degeneration, and not on their individual character:

> He was an extremely tall fellow, *unkempt* and *none too clean*, *gaunt* from undernourishment, with *sunken* chest and long, grasping hands. His face was *puffy*, his hair and beard, strongly *streaked with grey*, were *disheveled*; his voice was loud, but *hoarse and croaking*; his eyes *bulging and bloodshot*, partly from too much vodka, partly from being out in all weathers.

Clearly, physical manifestations interest Saltykov little except as a reflection of the characters' inner state (an important example of this is Porfirii's pious posturing). For the most part he presents the Golovlyovs through their conversations and through his own analytical commentary. Saltykov had a rare command of the many various tones of the Russian language and nowhere did he demonstrate this skill better than in his handling of conversation. In *The Golovlyov Family*, as in the satirical works, it is the conversations that stand out as the highlights. The core of the novel is a series of conversational duels between the main characters. Each character's speech has its own flavor – the richly expressive popular style of Arina Petrovna, the modish jargon of Stepan and Petia, the nauseatingly affected childishness of Porfirii. The conversations are entirely authentic, the different modes of speech are genuine, not mere stylizations. It is interesting that Saltykov almost always gives his conversations "raw." All that is essential is conveyed by the utterances alone, with little recourse to comments on gestures, glances, or tones of voice which, for example, Tolstoy so commonly used to dramatize conversations, as did Turgenev, Dostoevsky, and Chekhov to a lesser degree. Saltykov was confident, and rightly so, of his power to convey everything by his characters' words alone.

Saltykov is equally direct and forceful in his analytical passages describing the Golovlyovs. Again, in keeping with his publicistic manner, he does not write about his characters in a detached way. He states the truth about the Golovlyovs with a forthrightness worthy of the Golovlyovs themselves. His language is neither neutral nor restrained. "Judas," he declares, "was not so much a humbug as a mischief maker, a liar, and a blatherer." "Tears came into his [Porfirii's] eyes," he says, " – so well did he lie!" Saltykov mixes his own style with that of the Golovlyovs: he refers to Porfirii as "Judas" or "the bloodsucker" as casually as Stepan Golovlyov might; he mimics Porfirii's speech and his constant references to Arina Petrovna as "dear Mother" (*milyi drug mamen'ka*). Irony, which was Saltykov's supreme satirical weapon, appears in loaded paradoxes: he talks of Porfirii's "customary benignant manner in which it was quite impossible to tell whether he was about to do someone a favor or *suck his blood*," and refers to "those *brotherly* acts of baseness that came naturally to Porfirii." He describes "the *noble* looks, the *noble* manners, and the *noble* outlook" of Liul'kin (the zemstvo administrator who is Liubin'ka's protector) and adds that "all this together nonetheless convinced one that this was a man who, given half a chance, would make off with the zemstvo cash box."

The language of these sections is a bold mixture of varied elements – heavy literary language, bureaucratic and journalistic terms, biblical phrases and Church Slavonicisms mixed with often vulgar colloquialisms. Long rhetorical sentences are interspersed with vivid colloquial interjections. There is always an element of surprise in Saltykov's language, and it is the continual fluctuation of tone that prevents his often heavy prose from becoming ponderous.

Undoubtedly, the most impressive analytical passages are those describing the Golovlyovs in the final stages of decline before death.

The dull routine of idle days is described, days spent in aimless gazing from windows on bleak and empty landscapes, nights spent drinking and conjuring up the past. It is in such passages that the intensity of Saltykov's prose is seen most clearly. He uses strong vocabulary and a range of blatant rhetorical tricks (repetitions, inversions, rhetorical questions) to convey a powerful picture of the Golovlyovs' doomed state. He employs particularly words that express some absolute state or characteristic – "*hopeless loneliness*," "*powerless old age*," "*inescapable* thought," "*empty* space," "*completely dark*," "an *endless* succession of *dawnless* days *disappearing* in some yawning gray *abyss*." Typical of this "maximal" vocabulary, is the frequent use of adjectives and adverbs prefixed in Russian by *bez-/bes-* (equivalent in English to the prefix *un-* or the suffix *-less(ly)*). Typical, too, is the use of pronouns and adjectives such as "only," "all," "entire," "every," and cumulative negative statements expressing absolute conditions. Two passages can serve as illustrations.

> Such stirrings of . . . conscience are *unusually painful*. Without careful tending, seeing *no light* ahead, conscience brings *no reconciliation*, indicates *no possibility* of a new life. It is *only* a source of *endless, fruitless torment*. A man sees himself in a stone cell, *pitilessly* delivered over to the *agony of repentance*, to the *agony alone, without hope* of a return to life. And there is *no other way* of soothing the *fruitless consuming pain*, except the chance of using a moment of *grim* decision to dash out one's brains on the stone of the cell.

———

> He would wake with the morning light, and with him would wake *ennui, revulsion*, and *hate. Unprotesting, unfounded hate, hate* toward something *formless* and *undefined*. His bloodshot eyes stop *senselessly* on one object or another. . . . *Not a single* thought, *not a single* desire. Before him the stove – and he becomes so *obsessed* with this picture that his mind takes in *no other* impressions. Then the

window replaces the stove. *Window, window, window.* . . . There is *no need for anything, no need for anything, for anything at all.*

[The preceding extract is from a general article on *The Golovlyovs*, in which space did not allow detailed consideration of some important aspects of the novel. In the following remarks a closer look is taken at one of them: the means by which Saltykov characterizes Porfirii. – I. P. F.]

The creation of the character of Porfirii Golovlyov is one of Saltykov's greatest achievements as a writer. Saltykov was a practiced hand at presenting negative characters and his sketches are full of sharply observed cameo portraits of types representative of the imperfections of contemporary Russian life; it was only in the extended form of the novel that he had scope to develop a character in depth, and this he did successfully with Porfirii. Though far from objective, Saltykov's portrayal of his hero is psychologically consistent and convincing – and, it must be said, interesting and entertaining, for all the baseness of the character presented.

Saltykov achieves his characterization in four ways: his own analytical observations in the discursive passages relating to Porfirii that occur in every chapter from "Family Scores" on; Porfirii's deeds; descriptions of his physical features and gestures; and the ample record of his empty talk.

The discursive passages and Porfirii's actions need not be discussed. The former speak for themselves (and for Saltykov, who puts his stamp on them with his tendentious interjections) and are similar in kind to such expository passages devoted to other Golovlyov characters. Porfirii's "actions" are essentially confined to his treatment of other people, the victims of his dirty tricks and verbal tyranny, and this, too, is clear from the narrative episodes that make up the novel. Discussion will center, therefore, on Porfirii's physical presentation and the "rhetoric of humbug" that is the foundation of his empty talk.

That there is something sinister about Porfirii is indicated first in "Family Court" by references to how his family regards him: his mother half fears him; Stepan has dubbed him "Judas," "Bloodsucker," and "Candid Lad"; and there is the soothsayer's half-serious, half-comic forecast of trouble ahead for the mother hen from her latest offspring. The first direct manifestation of Porfirii's character comes not with his presence but with the obsequious letter that exemplifies the contrast between him and Pavel – significantly, it is by his *words* that his nature begins to be revealed. Thereafter, in the narrative sections, it is by physical reference and talk that the characterization is sustained.

Saltykov does not generally provide much detailed description of the physique and facial features of his characters; he is more concerned with what people are inwardly and how this expresses itself in their outward *condition*. It would be impossible from the information given to draw a clear picture of what Porfirii looks like: he is said to be "long and lean," on a couple of occasions he is "dressed (all) in black," and at the end he wears a tattered dressing gown (in keeping with his own decay). His facial features are not delineated, but Saltykov frequently refers to their *state*. At different times his face is said to be slavering, unctuous, green with malice; his lips quiver, blench, leer, smirk, twitch, twist, dribble, foam; his nose quivers with emotion, turns red from fervent praying; his eyes are oily, "take on an unctuous glaze," tears start in them, they seem (to Pavel) to exude venom and to cast a noose; his voice, too, is oily, unctuous, and seems (again to Pavel) to "slither like a snake into a man's soul." Sounds associated with him are subdued and sinister: he whispers his prayers, shuffles as he walks, hisses like a snake. His movements are furtive: he creeps, moves stealthily, walks on tiptoe, slips into doorways, appears suddenly and silently on thresholds. He peers, spies, and eavesdrops. Saltykov reports such features of Porfirii mostly in the course of the narrative; some are observed by the other characters: thus author and characters combine to create a repellent image. They share similarly in making denigrating associations between Porfirii and predatory creatures (animal and human) who act by stealth and guile: several times he is likened to a serpent, to a spider weaving a web, once (by Arina Petrovna) to a fox, to a snarer ("casting a noose"), and to an angler ("casting a line"). Another repeated image of a different sort is that of "dust" (*prakh* – "mortal dust," that is, suggesting his inner lifelessness): Evpraksiia sees him as a "coffinful of dust." These reiterated negative features and images – unrelieved by any more positive – are effective enough in establishing Porfirii as a repulsive figure, but they provide little hard evidence on which to base conclusions about his individual character; they could well portray *any* dastardly villain of melodrama. A serious assessment of Porfirii can only be based on the author's account given in the analytical passages and on the revelation of Porfirii's inward self that comes from his own empty talk. Porfirii's empty talk has two functions: it is a means by which he dominates others and it serves him as a barrier to block out the realities of normal life. Much of the book is taken up with his endless trivial discourses, and readers might well be as disheartened by them as are the other characters in the novel, that is if they were not left marveling at the verbal resourcefulness displayed in them. How is Porfirii's artistry of empty talk achieved?

Porfirii's speech is based chiefly on a system of forms and simple rhetorical constructions, the very repetition of which contribute to the tedium of what he says. The main lexical resource he exploits is peculiarly Russian and impossible to convey adequately in translation. This is the adaptation of words (mainly nouns, but also adjectives and adverbs) by a variety of suffixes which, without changing the meaning of the word, impart an emotional tone – affectionate, familiar, scornful – or, in the case of some, indicate size ("augmentative," "diminutive" function). There is usually a certain homeliness in these suffixes (and in their sound – *-ik, -ka, -ishka, -ushka, -ochka,* etc.), and words so adapted are common in informal speech among familiars and are used especially in talking to or among children. It would be natural, for instance, for someone like Arina Petrovna to use such forms when talking to Evpraksiia or her domestics. What is peculiar to Porfirii's speech is the excessive use he makes of these words; we find, for instance, in his conversation with Arina Petrovna on the discomforts of being outside and the comforts of being inside during a blizzard (in "Family Scores"), some forty of them in a single page, including "double" suffixes in certain nouns (e.g., *laptishechki* 'bast shoes', from *lapti* via *laptishki*) and adverbs (e.g., *svetlëkhon'ko* 'light', from *svetlo* via *svetlen'ko*) and unusual formations from foreign words (*proviziitsy* 'provisions', from *provizii*). The accumulation of these suffixed words in his speech suggests a benign homeliness, which of course contrasts with Porfirii's true, malignant nature. The same effect is created by his use of verb forms characteristic of popular speech, especially verbs prefixed by *po-* (usually the prefix conveys the idea of "doing a bit" of whatever action the verb refers to): *popit'* ('to drink'), *poest'* ('to eat'), *polakomit'sya* ('to have a tasty bite'), and so on. Verbs may be prefixed by *po-* and add the suffix *-ivat'* (or *-yvat'*) which gives a nuance of "iterative" action, again without altering the basic sense of the root verb. Such forms tend to have a "folksy" ring and Porfirii uses them frequently – juxtaposed, as in *metel' povizgivaet* (*vizzhit*), *a my chaёk popivaem* (*p'ëm*) 'the storm howls away but we drink our tea', or joined in a tautological pair with the root verb, as in *vizzhit da povizgivaet* 'howls and howls away', *katai da pokatyvai* 'ride and ride'.

Analogous to the above in their homely effect are the proverbial sayings (the store of "ready-made aphorisms") Porfirii uses in his moralizing and the stock phrases to which he so frequently has recourse – such sayings as *Pospeshish'* – *liudei nasmeshish'* 'Hurry and you make a fool of yourself', *Sam naputal* – *sam i vyputyvaisia* 'You got yourself into the mess, you get yourself out of it', and his motto phrases like *tikho da smirno* 'slow and steady', *mirkom da ladkom* 'in peace and harmony', *ne toropias', da Bogu pomolias'* 'making no haste and praying God's good grace'. In these, as in some of the purely lexical features described, there is often rhyme, rhythm, and assonance which give a distinct, almost poetic color to Porfirii's speech; for all the banality of what he says, his mastery of the spoken Russian word has to be acknowledged.

The rhetorical devices Porfirii uses are, for the most part, the kind that induces tedium. These include:

1. *Repetition* (with or without lexical variation): "Have some rest, have some comfort, have some sleep. Then we'll talk, think things over, weigh it up"; "Oh, what a mistake that was! Oh, such a mistake, such a mistake!"; "With truth I was born, with truth I have lived, with truth I shall die."

2. *Listing*: [At the foundlings' home there are] "nice clean little cots, good healthy wet-nurses, nice white little shirts for the babies, feeding bottles, teats, napkins" (the ten Russian words in this list *all* have affective suffixes – *krovatki*, *chisten'kie*, etc.); [We drink tea] "with sugar and with cream and with lemon. And if we want it with rum, we have it with rum"; [Of estate routine]: "This to look at, that to see to, a call to be made there, a word here, a word there."

3. *Definitive statements, introduced by a question*: "What are children? Children are . . . "; "What will God say to this? God will say . . . "; "What does the Scripture say about patience? In patience possess ye your souls, it says."

4. *Contrasting statements* ("A as opposed to B"): "One merit is great, another merit is small"; [During the blizzard]: "Bad for some, but no matter to us. Some are out in the dark and cold, but we're cosy [here] in the light and warm."

5. *Contrasting propositions* ("If A then B, if not A then C (or not B)"): "If there's need of anything, we'll see to it, and if there's no need, we'll just sit"; "If you ask for what's right, you shall have it . . . But if you ask for what's not right – too bad!"

6. *Augmentation and reduction*: "If there's need to go five miles, I'll go five miles; or if it's ten miles, I'll go ten miles."; "A rouble here, a half-rouble there, a quarter there."

These devices are all *extensive* in the sense that they give Porfirii the opportunity to go on at length, to say, effectively, the same thing twice. Since he talks mainly in platitudes, the wearing effect of this on his listeners is the more assured. Porfirii's manner is usually declarative. Though he is happy to engage in small talk with Arina Petrovna, he comes into his own when he "holds forth" with some moralizing rigmarole. Once launched, he allows no interruption; he rebukes even Arina Petrovna when she attempts to interrupt while he is speaking (it is a sign of his approaching decline when, in "Escheated," Evpraksiia succeeds in bringing his outpourings to a halt by her complaints and interruptions). He is rarely put to developing an argument at any length, but he acquits himself well when he does; among his most masterly performances are his justification for sending the baby Volodka to the foundlings' home (to Ulita, in "Illicit Family Joys") and his self-exculpatory denunciation of Evpraksiia for fornication (to the priest, in the same chapter).

In the last pages of "The Reckoning" Porfirii drops his verbal mask and speaks in words of true feeling. His broken statements and questions to Annin'ka complete a notable piece of characterization achieved through the spoken word.

A Classic of Russian Realism: Form and Meaning in *The Golovlyovs*

MILTON EHRE

If not for *The Golovlyovs* Mikhail Saltykov (pen name N. Shchedrin, hence Saltykov-Shchedrin) (1826–1889) would be remembered today as a journalist of considerable talent and intelligence who, along with several other men of letters – Herzen, the poet Nekrasov, the critic Chernyshevsky – embodied the conscience of radical Russia in the nineteenth century. He was a writer of satires, often topical and ephemeral, only occasionally rising to the universality of enduring art. In his satires Saltykov's strengths are a gift for parody, complemented by a fine ear for the nuances of the diverse stylistic levels of the Russian language, a vivid imagination for the grotesque – reminiscent, at its best, of Swift, and owing much to Gogol – and an authentic moral outrage at injustice. His weaknesses are endemic to Russian journalism of the nineteenth century, which was conducted in polemical heat by men anxious to persuade and disdaining artfulness as a luxury ill-afforded in suffering Russia. Saltykov is often prolix, obvious, even painfully crude. The Aesopian code he devised to outwit the censors is sometimes obscure, and many of his sallies against contemporary figures have otherwise lost their edge. His books are usually compilations of occasional journalistic pieces lacking cohesion and tied together only by a common subject – the corruption of provincial officials, the rapacious greed of the new bourgeoisie, the ineffectuality of well-intentioned liberals (a favorite target). Wildly overpraised in the Soviet Union, the satires have been ignored in the West. Serious readers of Russian literature agree, however, that *The Golovlyovs*, Saltykov's only true novel, is a classic of Russian realistic fiction.

It is a somber and grim book – "the gloomiest in all Russian literature,"[1] Mirsky called it. A nineteenth-century family novel, it tells the story of the disintegration of a family of the Russian provincial gentry – the Golovlyovs – which is implicitly the story of the decline of their class. Like Saltykov's satires, the novel is virtually "plotless," if we understand plot in the conventional sense of a story arranged so as to arouse curiosity about impending events. The first two chapters introduce a situation that might have developed into such a plot. Arina Petrovna, the imperious matriarch of the kingdom of Golovlyovo, divides her estate, giving the lion's share to the most vicious of her sons – the greedy Porfirii, or, as he is called, "Little Judas" and "Bloodsucker." The motif is common to folklore and familiar to all of us from *Lear* – the folklorish overtones are in the novel but in parodic, not portentous, accents. But Arina's act fails to generate a sustained plot. It hardly would have made any difference in the Golovlyovs' fortunes had she divided her estate otherwise, bequeathing the better parts to her sons Pavel and Stepan, who are incompetents and alcoholics. Plots grow out of the motives and choices of characters leading to action in the context of circumstance. The Golovlyovs are dimly aware of the changing circumstances of their lives – the emancipation of the serfs, the disaffection of the young from the old patriarchal traditions, the familial enmities that are tearing them apart. Confronted by the imperatives of history, they remain essentially passive. As a result, the novel gives the impression, an intended one, of men and women driven by an inner fatality and subject to impersonal forces beyond their control. Their actions, such as they are, continually turn into meaningless gestures before an implacable destiny.

The absence of "plot" and the looseness of form of Saltykov's work did not stem from lack of literary culture – a charge often leveled against Russian novelists of the nineteenth century. To write so was a conscious and deliberate choice. Those "fluid puddings" and "baggy monsters," to invoke Henry James's famous but misplaced epithets, reflected a widely held aesthetic position. The Realists – not only the Russians, though the attitude was particularly strong among them – viewed plot and tightly knit form as smacking of artfulness and artificiality. Ingenuity of plot construction belonged properly to the inventiveness of the Romantics; "plots" could only obfuscate the rendering of "real life." The Realistic urge was pictorial instead of dramatic. Also plots tend to individualize. Through them we become caught up in the destiny of one or several individuals struggling against circumstances, and we eagerly await the outcome. It was Saltykov's intention in *The Golovlyovs*, not merely to tell a story, but, as in the satires, to present a series of portraits that would culminate in a consummate image of Russian life. He considered Gogol his teacher and, as in *Dead Souls*, the artist's concentration is on the evocation of a total cosmos.[2]

This is not to say that *The Golovlyovs* lacks form. It grew, as did the satires, out of a series of sketches, but in the process of writing Saltykov discovered, perhaps under the promptings of his excited readers, that he had a novel. Where many of the satires accumulated into "cycles," as Russian criticism calls them, over a period of many years *The Golovlyovs*, except for the final chapter that serves as an epilogue, was written in a relatively brief time span – from July 1875 through November 1876. Saltykov made extensive changes, including transposing chapters and making excisions and additions, for a separate edition of 1880 and again for a second edition in 1883. These technical adjustments were necessary and important. The germ of a novel was there from the beginning, and those readers, among them Turgenev and Goncharov, who urged him to continue, felt it (Goncharov and others even offered possible endings).[3] *The Golovlyovs*, as it appeared in the journal *Notes of the Fatherland* and, more so, in its final version, displays a consistency of tone and concentration of vision that make it all of a piece. As such it holds a unique place in Saltykov's oeuvre, too much of which breaks down into scattered shots taken at topical objects of indignation. Its intensity of focus may have much to do with the fact that, despite its generalizing intentions, it is a profoundly personal book. It is Saltykov's portrait of the provincial Russian he knew so well, but it is also an attempt to purge himself of the ghosts of his past. The

Golovlyovs, in heightened and exaggerated form, no doubt, were the Saltykovs.[4]

Though much of the novel is pictorial, presenting a gallery of grotesque portraits of the Russian gentry in the senseless rounds of daily routine, it is not static and its scenes do not remain disconnected. The "action" of the novel – to distinguish from conventional plot – that is, what gives it its shape and force, lies in a series of accounts of the moral and physical disintegration of each of the Golovlyovs. The principle of organization is rhythmic instead of dramatic. The opening introduces us to the cast of characters – all the Golovlyovs who figure importantly save one, a granddaughter named Annin'ka – and then renders in vivid, often harrowing detail their successive descents into oblivion. "They are picked up at the moment in their lives when the dénouement begins to take shape, at the moment when they lose . . . hope," as one writer put it.[5] Come to us out of the final act of a tragedy of which the other acts have been excised, the Golovlyovs have no other recourse but to slide downhill. The true movement of the novel, what gives it its awesome fascination, lies in the continuing flights of its characters into the abyss. Literary modes have psychological analogues, and the manner of *The Golovlyovs* is obsessive. The narrative becomes riveted on these disintegrations of character and the interludes are moments of preparation for the inevitable. The accounts of the successive falls, all of them similar, introduce, in the absence of a controlling plot, a rhythm of presentation – a series of analogical curves sweeping downward from the stasis of everyday life.

The curves overlap, establishing continuity in a book that threatens to break down, like Saltykov's other writings, into a series of sketches, but never does. The story of Stepan's disintegration in the first chapter sets the pattern of the book. While telling it, Saltykov deftly foreshadows Pavel's similar doom – "I see you want to follow Stepka's footsteps," Arina says to him, and his distracted air, the "disconnected words" he speaks, as if he were talking "through a dream" (40), informs us that he is a carbon copy of his brother. Arina is at the height of her powers in chapter 1, an absolute monarch in her tiny kingdom. But power for Saltykov is a kind of fatality. In the case of Arina, as later of Judas, it isolates the individual from family and community, provokes anxiety over the thought of its loss, and self-pity lest its exertions go misunderstood. Those who hold it live in constant need of reassurance and self-justification. Arina, even at the moment of her supremacy, feels herself slipping into the decrepitude of old age, and despairs that the legacy of her reign will prove empty: "For whom have I been saving it all! . . . for whom?" (44) she cries, and the cry resounds through the novel. It never takes long for the people of Golovlyovo to fall. Though the narrator on occasion intervenes to tell us that a number of years have passed, the reigns of power, because their dissolutions are so abrupt, seem to transpire in a moment. In chapter 2 Arina flees to another lesser estate, Dubrovino to wait for death, abandoning the family manor to Judas the Bloodsucker.

In one of the many intimations of things to come in chapter 1, Stepan predicted that Judas would destroy "the old witch" and "suck" her property out of her (24), and in chapter 2 Porfirii takes over. However, where Arina had the ingrained posture of power, Judas is its caricature. His unctuous moralizing parodies traditional Russian piety, and his exaggerated civility caricatures the gentility of a Russian aristocrat. At times his language falls into a degraded bureaucratese – Porfirii has just retired from a career in the civil service. He is obviously intended as a consummate image of the Russian gentry, incorporating its traditional double role as master of the manor and government official, as well as its double heritage of Byzantine religiosity and post-Petrine bureaucratism. Often compared to Tartuffe and perhaps patterned on him in part, Porfirii also echoes the grotesque marionettes who rule the Town of Fools that is Russia in Saltykov's best satire, *History of a Town*, his mock allegory of Russian history. His arrival to assume possession of Dubrovino reads like a parody of the coronation of a Russian ruler:

Slowly, solemnly he got out of the carriage, waved off the servants who were hurtling forward to kiss the master's hands, then folded his hands with the palms turned in and leisurely climbed the stairs, whispering a prayer. His face expressed both sorrow and determined resignation. . . . His sons, walking side by side, followed him. Volodenka mimicked his father; he folded his hands, rolled his eyes, moved his lips. Petenka enjoyed the performance. The cortege of servants followed in a silent crowd.

Judas kissed his mamma on the hand, then on the lips, then again on the hand.

"You're so downcast! That's not nice, my darling! Oh, it's not nice! Just ask yourself: ask, what would God say to that? Well, He would say: here, in My infinite wisdom I arrange everything for the best, and she's complaining! Oh, mamma! mamma!" (74).

The images of power Saltykov presents in the first two chapters of *The Golovlyovs* are ordered, as everything else in the novel, to present a picture of progressive weakening: from the imperious Arina who possesses the instinct to rule and yet has begun to feel and fear the ravages of mortality, to Porfirii who is a caricature of that rule, to the sons for whom his tyranny is impotent and ludicrous. It comes as no surprise when in the succeeding chapters we discover Porfirii losing his grip on those around him and ultimately, as happens to all the Golovlyovs, his hold on reality.

Thus, except for the story of the granddaughter Annin'ka, all the important Golovlyov disasters – those of Arina and those of her three sons, Stepan, Pavel, and Porfirii – are told or prepared in the first two chapters. Of these the tales of Arina and Porfirii – the mistress of Golovlyovo and her surviving heir – dominate. They divide the novel symmetrically: Arina dies in the middle chapter (4); Porfirii in the last chapter (7). Another symmetrical frame is formed by the parallel stories of the two Golovlyov offspring, the son Stepan and the granddaughter, who return to die after misadventures in the larger world – Stepan in the first chapter, Annin'ka in the final one. The dominant images of the novel are of darkness and death – the entire world is "a coffin"; Golovlyovo is "death itself" (119, 249) – and the novel itself is organized around dying. Dying is the true action of *The Golovlyovs*. As a result, the pressures of actual circumstance ebb into insignificance. The novel does not end because the lines of a plot have been tied together and its entanglements resolved. It ends simply because its rhythms have been exhausted. The Golovlyovs fade one by one, and when there are none – as in the child's jingle of the ten little Indians – the book is over.

Its last sentence introduced a new Golovlyov, a distant relation "who has been keeping a sharp eye on everything happening in Golovlyovo." Apparently the pattern of possession and dispossession, of power gained and power lost that characterized the lives of Arina and Judas is to continue after their deaths. But though power may continue to be the reigning impulse of human life, the reader, in putting down *The Golovlyovs*, knows that the context of its exercise had to change, for Saltykov has painted a persuasive portrait of a society where authority has lost conviction and life is without substance. *The Golovlyovs* stands with Goncharov's *Oblomov*, Bunin's *Dry Valley*, Chekhov's *Cherry Orchard* as one of the great Russian literary epitaphs on a dying social order.

A novel without "plot," built on repeated and highly similar patterns, could easily become tedious. Fortunately, *The Golovlyovs* is a short novel, for it is doubtful whether Saltykov could have sustained his achievement at much greater length. Within its pages, for perhaps the only time in his career, he maintained a thorough consistency of vision. His hold over his characters is total. The narrative voice, except for a few minor lapses into didacticism, is authoritative. Saltykov had cultivated a cool and logical narrative style – a frequent trait of the satirist – and "the tone of a systematic investigator"[6] serves to keep the chaos of Golovlyovo at a distance. The language of the dialogues is one of the triumphs of Russian literature. In a novel empty of dramatic action, verbal gestures function, along with narrative exposition, as major indicators of character. The language of dialogue takes full advantage, as do few nineteenth-century works of prose, of the richness of colloquial Russian. The language of Judas the Bloodsucker, in particular, is "so striking that the reader must pause to admire it for its own perfection."[7] Saltykov crams his speech with emotionally nuanced affixes, either pejorative or affectionate, to catch his wheedling, insinuating, complaining character – hardly a word he speaks is in the normative form – and lards it with folk proverbs and maxims, expressive of the stereotyped moralizing of this Russian Tartuffe. The spoken language of the novel is both mimetic and satiric, catching, on the one hand, the rhythms of common speech, and, on the other, inflating them to illustrate what is one of its larger themes – the degradation even of language in Golovlyovo.[8]

Though consistency of tone is essential in giving *The Golovlyovs* its coherence, the novel achieves its compelling force and its true rhythm in the periodic descents of its characters into oblivion. These are rendered with psychological acuity and perfect verisimilitude. Saltykov brings to bear on them a dispassionateness of manner that avoids any trace of sentimentality and yet never becomes coldly clinical. Much of the effect comes from long accumulations of careful perceptions that slowly draw us into the madness of his characters. They cannot be reproduced in entirety, but an excerpt of some length may be instructive, for Saltykov must have felt, when he decided to build his novel around successive disintegrations of his people, that we would know them by their illnesses. I take as my example the collapse of Stepan in chapter 1. His life a muddle, Stepan returns to Golovlyovo where he fears to go and yet, like all the Golovlyovs, feels irresistibly drawn[9] He walks up to the family manor muttering to himself, "Coffin! Coffin! Coffin!" "The doors of the tomb open, let him in, and bang shut," and his life resolves into "a stream of dull, formless days, sinking one after another into the gray, yawning abyss of time."

The future, hopeless and inescapable, . . . with each day became more and more enveloped in mist and, finally, altogether ceased to exist. The urgent present, in its cynical nakedness, came to the fore, came so insistently and brazenly that it entirely filled his thoughts, his entire being.

. . . . the gray, forever lachrimose autumn sky oppressed him.

It seemed to be suspended directly over his head, threatening to drown him in the gaping abysses of the earth. He had nothing to do but look through the window and watch the heavy masses of clouds. . . . the entire horizon was densely overcast; clouds stood as if frozen, spellbound; an hour passed, then a second, a third, and they still stood in the same place without the slightest, perceptible change in color or shape. There that cloud, the one that's lower and blacker than the rest, a while back it had a ragged shape . . . – and now, at noon, it has kept the same shape . . . – and rain pours from it, pours so that even against the dark canvas of the sky, an even darker, almost black band appears. And there, yet another cloud further on: a while ago it hung like a huge shaggy lump over the neighboring village of Naglovka and threatened to smother it – and now it still hangs over the same spot, the same shaggy lump, stretching its paws downward, as if about to pounce. Clouds, clouds, clouds . . . the landscape steadily clouds over, clouds over, and finally disappears altogether. At first the clouds vanish into an indistinct black film; then the forest disappears and Naglovka; then the church, the chapel, the nearby peasant settlement, and the orchard sink into it . . . [in] a process of mysterious disappearances. . . . The room was darkened completely; . . . he could only pace, pace, pace without end. A sickly lassitude paralyzed his mind; he felt . . . a groundless, inexpressible weariness spreading through his entire body. Only one thought tossed through his brain, sucked at it, crushed it: coffin! coffin! coffin!

. . . His dulled imagination struggled to form images, his deadened memory tried to break through into the territory of his past. But the images came out broken, inane, and the past did not yield a single memory, bright or bitter, as if once and for all a thick blank wall had arisen between it and the present. The present alone was before him in the form of this tightly locked prison from which the concept of space and the concept of time had disappeared without leaving a trace. The room, the stove, the three windows in the wall, the squeaky wooden bed with its thin flattened mattress, the table with the bottle standing on it – his thoughts could not reach to any other horizons. But . . . even this meager sense of the present proved beyond his capacity. His muttering . . . disintegrated completely; his pupils dilated beyond measure, straining to distinguish the outlines of the darkness; then the darkness itself vanished, and in its stead a space filled with a phosphorescent glow appeared. It was an infinite void, dead, without a single sound of life, ominously luminous. . . . Walls, windows, nothing existed; only this glowing void, stretching boundlessly. . . .

. . . He woke at dawn. . . . His inflamed eyes rested senselessly now on one object, now another, looking at them long and fixedly. . . . Not a single thought, not a single desire. The stove was before his eyes, and its image completely filled his mind, so that it could not receive any other impression. Then the window replaced the stove; it was window, window, window. He needs nothing, nothing, nothing. . . . It's best to sit and be quiet, be quiet and stare at one spot. . . . He must wait for the night in order again to break through to those blissful moments when the earth disappears from under his feet and, instead of four hateful walls, the boundless glowing void opens before his eyes. (30–31, 47–50)

The episode had begun with a summary of Stepan's failed life, so that the process of narration is from the telling of the story of a life in time to the point where time collapses, from history to the end of history. The past is forgotten, the future, which was constructed out of hopes and dreams, disappears, and time dissolves into an eternal present of "dawnless days," "formless" and indistinguishable. As time contracts to the infinitesimal present, space also shrinks. Heavy gray masses of clouds press down on Stepan, confine and oppress him, the landscape melts away, people, in part of the passage we have excluded, turn into dots, and finally Stepan finds himself in his coffinlike room, alone with brute objects – a stove, a bed, a window. The cataloguelike accumulations of things; the lingering on imagery – "the cloud hung like a huge shaggy lump . . . , now it still hangs over the same spot, the same shaggy lump"; the parallelisms and doublings – "there, that cloud . . . , and there yet another," "sucked at it, crushed it," "not a single thought, not a single desire"; and above all the pounding repetitions – "clouds, clouds, clouds," "window, window, window," the rain that "pours . . . , pours," the sky that "clouds over, clouds over," Stepan, who is only able "to pace, to pace, to pace" – all combine to create a passage of extreme density and insistency. Though the novel shows movement in its periodic descents into the abyss, what it moves to are conditions of perfect stasis – a nature that is "frozen" and "spellbound," a society that is a "coffin." The style apprehends this stasis through its dwelling upon mute, dead objects, or frozen attitudes. It is as possessed by things as is Stepan's tormented brain. Again, it is an obsessive style, hammering at the mind of the reader, as things hammer at the mind of Stepan.

The radical tradition to which Saltykov adhered, under the sway of mid-century positivism, regarded "reality," or the realm of material objects and circumstances, as an ultimate value. For the Golovlyovs such a reality is the ultimate horror. What makes their reality horrible is its narrowness. On the one hand, it has become unhinged from the dimension of time, so that the moments of experience are no longer part of a larger historical process proceeding from a known, or at least knowable, past to a conceivable future. On the other hand, reality has become reduced to what the Latin root of the word says – things. The reality of Golovlyovo is empty of emotional content and devoid of spiritual value. Lacking adequate contexts of meaning and value, the Golovlyovs stand before an incoherence of things, a reality turned into nightmare. Stepan's madness reflects Golovlyovo at a heightened and extreme moment – though each of its inhabitants sinks into something like it – but it is not far removed from "normal" Golovlyovo. The madness of its characters stands as a great metaphor for a world where minds are possessed by money, food rots in storehouses while children go hungry, and the collective consciousness is dominated by things.

The style of mental life in Golovlyovo is what today we would call "paranoid." Freud, in his classic paper on paranoia, describes its primary event as a withdrawing of emotion from people and objects in the external world (people in Stepan's perceptions become "dots"; he stares at the things before him "long and fixedly" without "a single thought," "a single desire"). The delusional systems accompanying paranoia are for Freud attempts "*of reconstruction*" of relations "to people and things" in a world grown dead.[10] In the world of Golovlyovo, which is "death itself" (249), paranoid delusions run wild. Stepan fears that his brother Judas the Bloodsucker has the power to crawl into his soul (24). Arina, in a passage remarkably similar to the one quoted above, finds time collapsing, the landscape fading into mist, her thoughts become disconnected and her mind turns to ruminating over old insults and terrors of "thieves, apparitions, devils" (96–97). Pavel, who also fears Judas's "snakelike" capacity to crawl into another's skin and exude a "spellbinding venom" to paralyze the will, constructs elaborate fantasies – "an entire mock-heroic novel" – in which Judas is the victim, he the aggressor made invincible by magical powers of invisibility (66–67). Judas, who is the object of everyone's fear, in the end comes to fear everyone and everything. His religion had always been pure demonology, his prayer an intricate ritualism devised to ward off evil spirits. When he collapses, "the earth disappears from under his feet," "people become dehumanized," and "his unlimited imagination creates an imaginary reality" of megalomaniacal power in which he is able to avenge all the insults he has suffered in his life, and to walk the dead earth invisible and impervious to harm (216–19). Whatever there is of plot in the novel turns on dispossession – of property and inheritance – and its psychological analogue is dispossession of the self – an emptying of the subjective world projected outward as the disintegration of the objective world of time and space. Lost in this emptiness, the Golovlyovs fabricate those petty dramas of persecution and revenge that the paranoid mind contrives as a desperate substitute for real life.

But for all the profundity of Saltykov's psychological observation, his ultimate interest is not psychological but, as in all his work, sociological. Critics, especially in the Soviet Union, have pointed to the emancipation of the serfs, which takes place in the course of the novel, as the crucial historical fact determining the Golovlyovs' fate. The old patriarchal ways fail to bind the community as they once did: Arina loses heart for the business of management, the free peasants avoid working for Judas because they cannot stand his ceaseless jabbering, his housekeeper and mistress, a former serf, rebels. But the old habits of idleness and dependency persist and make the Golovlyovs incapable of administering the estate to meet new economic conditions as well as unfit for any other occupation; the story of Annin'ka's corruption in the demimonde of Bohemia before her inevitable return to Golovlyovo at least to die "a mistress" dramatizes the point.

But Saltykov's critique of Russian life runs much deeper than this. *The Golovlyovs* leaves a searing impression of the poverty of Russian culture, or at least the culture of its ruling class. In a brief essay inserted into the text Saltykov compares French and Russian society. He experienced the love-hate relation to France of the Russian radical intelligentsia, inspired by its revolutionary traditions and repelled by its bourgeois complacency. The latter attitude came to the fore after the failures of the 1848 Revolution. In his essay Saltykov sees French society as characterized by hypocrisy, but when we look closely we discern that what he calls hypocrisy might just as easily be labeled convention: "In France hypocrisy is cultivated by upbringing; it forms, one may say, a part of good manners." The hypocrisy of the French is "an inducement to decency, to decorum, to elegant appearances; most important of all, hypocrisy is – is a restraint." On the other hand, "we Russians have no powerfully elaborated systems of upbringing. . . . we are simply left to grow, as nettles grow by a fence. . . . We have no need to be hypocritical about social principles, for we don't know any such principles. . . . We exist completely free, that is, we vegetate, lie, and chatter emptily according to our tastes, without any concern for principles" (101–3). The opposition setting French social man, bound by "hypocrisy" or convention, against the Russian anarchical soul was a favorite one of the Russian

nineteenth century, especially among romantic Slavophiles. As Saltykov's novel subverts those idealizations of the manorial estate common in Russian literature – the frequently idyllic landscapes of Aksakov, Turgenev, Tolstoy – it explodes the romantic myth of natural
innocence. His "natural" Russian lives in a Hobbesian state of nature
where life is "solitary, poor, nasty, brutish," though not always short.
The estate, for Saltykov, has determined the paradoxical "freedom"
of the Russian. It has shaped a society that isolates men in provincial
enclaves cut off from intercourse with the larger world, and has
allowed some of them to indulge capricious whims and arbitrary
power. The world of Golovlyovo offers no limits for unbridled fantasy. Even nature has conspired against the Russian. The usual landscapes of the novel are bleak and empty: the mind roves over "fields,
fields without end," "naked, infinite fields," thoughts become "torn,"
they have nothing to hold on to, memories break into "fragments
. . . without connection" (96). Where the French novel from Sten-
dhal to Proust mirrors the individual in an intricate matrix of social
convention, Saltykov's characters, like those of many Russian writers,
again especially Gogol's, bear the burden of emptiness.

Conventions are modes of providing "connections," of ordering
experience. They grow out of the shared histories of people. They
can be, as Saltykov says, elaborate hypocrisies used by the privileged
to rationalize their power, but they are also, he adds, though
grudgingly, the cement of society; hypocrisy (or convention) is "an
inducement to decency" and, like law, "a restraint." The Russians of
Saltykov's fictional world live without the necessary restraints of
social convention and have been severed from those historical experiences that might justify the acceptance of such conventions. I said
earlier that Saltykov built his book so that we would know his characters by their illnesses. What we learn about them as they go to
pieces is that they have lost the past. Undoubtedly they have lost it
because they do not want it, because it offers nothing but memories
of niggardliness, hate, and mean struggles for power. But without it
they lack that store of historical experience from which men and
nations extract meaning. The people of Golovlyovo are doomed to

historical imbecility: "[Stepan's] deadened memory tried to break through into the territory of his past. But the image came out broken, inane, and the past did not yield a single memory, bright or bitter, as if once and for all a thick blank wall had arisen between it and the present. The present alone was before him in the form of this tightly locked prison." The Golovlyovs, without "principles" to order experience, without historical memories to place it in a larger context, find themselves in a space composed of senseless objects, in a time reduced to the narrow, present instant. This is their "prison."

Because their minds become emptied of vital content, the Golovlyovs turn into straws tossed about helplessly by historical forces beyond their control or victims passively suffering mortal decay. Ultimately, however, Saltykov is not a determinist but a moralist of Russian cloth. There remains one shred of consciousness his people cannot extinguish in themselves, try as they may – their consciousness of their guilt. Their guilt furnishes the only fragments of memory they cannot fully exorcise. It helps explain the fatalistic submissiveness with which the children of Golovlyovo return to the hated familial nest, like lemmings rushing blindly to their death, for what they at times seem to be seeking is punishment.[11] Guilt also exercises a positive function. For more pastoral temperaments guilt is something to flee; for sterner minds like Saltykov's it is the source of conscience. Golovlyovo becomes a house haunted by "gray ghosts," and what the ghosts speak of is a past of "drunkenness, fornication, torment, streaming blood" – a past that at "the slightest touch produced pain" (256). The "awakenings of neglected conscience" among the Golovlyovs appear only at the moment of total destitution; Saltykov's distaste for power is total. The awakenings do not last, and conscience does not save them. The Christian allusions to Easter and Resurrection at the conclusion remain one of the few moments in the novel that fail to convince.[12] What does convince is the pain. It is the triumph of this novel that the gallery of grotesques which Saltykov has given us – these men and women driven by extravagances of avarice and envy, indifferent to one another and to themselves – come across to us as oddly human, in their moments of

pain, pathetically so. Saltykov, like every Russian writer of his generation, rejected French Naturalism for its failure to present "the *whole*
man" in the manner of the Russian Realists.[13] There are no whole
men in Saltykov's fictional world, but those flickers of conscience his
characters perceive serve to remind us that they, and not society or
nature alone, have been at fault. Potentially, though never actually,
they are free moral beings.

The sense of a lost past, of living without a history, ran deep in
Russian consciousness of the nineteenth century. A line from Peter
Chaadaev's scandalous "First Letter on the Philosophy of History"
(1836) could stand as an epigraph to *The Golovlyovs*: "We live entirely
in the present in its narrowest confines, without a past or future,
amid a dead calm."[14] The poverty of Russian history was for the
intelligentsia a paradoxical source of hope, since it meant that Russia
could start anew with a clean slate. As Herzen put it, "Nous sommes
moralement plus libres que les européens, . . . parce que nous
n'avons pas de passé qui nous maîtrise." [We are morally more free
than the Europeans because we have no past to curb us].[15] Sometimes Russians made their past seem poorer than it actually was by
minimizing the considerable accomplishments of Russian culture, so
that we find Belinsky bemoaning the absence of a Russian literature
after the Golden Age of Pushkin, and Merezhkovsky, a half century
later, complaining of the lack of a Russian literary culture after a
century that had given the world Pushkin, Gogol, Dostoevsky,
Tolstoy.[16] The reverse side of this crisis of national self-confidence
can be found in Slavophile inventions of a glorious mythical past
existing only in their imaginations. Saltykov, though he mouthed the
usual nineteenth-century shibboleths of progress and enlightenment
and at times seemed to share the Populist faith in the simplicity,
virtue, and strength of the peasantry, was by constitution too much
the debunker, and in his art too much the satirist, to commit himself
fully to easy solutions. Herzen (who also had his moments of skepti-
cism), cheered by the vista of a Russia unburdened by the past, where
men could, like God, create from nothing, was fond of quoting
Goethe's famous lines celebrating an America also free from the

constraints of tradition: "Amerika, du hast es besser." [America, you are better off]. In Saltykov's masterpiece the alienation of men from their history is the seed of their destruction. "Russland, du hast es schlimmer" [Russia, you are worse off] is what the novel, and indeed Saltykov's entire corpus, cries out to us.

NOTES

1. D. S. Mirsky, *A History of Russian Literature*, 2d ed. (New York: Knopf, 1949), 281.

2. See his remarks on the novel as a genre, in S. Balukhatyi et al., eds., *Russkie pisateli o literature* (Leningrad: Sovetskii pisatel', 1939), 2:222–23.

3. The history of composition and publication and variants of the text may be found in M. E. Saltykov-Shchedrin, *Sobranie sochinenii*, vol. 13 (Moscow: Khudozhestvennaia literatura, 1972), 565–694 (references to *The Golovlyovs* are to this volume). Though translations are largely my own, I have made use of *The Golovlovs*, trans. Andrew R. MacAndrew (New York: New American Library, 1961). Turgenev's reaction is in *Polnoe sobranie sochinenii i pisem: Pis'ma* (Moscow-Leningrad: Nauka, 1961–67), 11:149; Goncharov's is in *Sobranie sochinenii* (Moscow: Khudozhestvennaia literatura, 1952–55), 8:489–91.

4. The parallels are apparent to readers of his interesting fictionalized auto-biography, *Poshekhonskaia starina* (Old times in Poshekhonie). See also S. Makashin, *Saltykov-Shchedrin*, 2d ed. (Moscow: Khudozhestvennaia literatura, 1951), 11–72.

5. Kyra Sanine, *Saltykov-Chtchédrine: sa vie et ses oeuvres* (Paris: Institut d'études slaves de l'Université de Paris, 1955), 223.

6. Ia. El'sberg, *Stil' Shchedrina* (Moscow: Khudozhestvennaia literatura, 1940), 203.

7. William E. Harkins, afterword to MacAndrew, trans., *The Golovlovs*, 315. Harkins's afterword is the best essay on the novel I have found.

8. These effects are untranslatable. For helpful studies, see El'sberg, and A. I. Efimov, *Iazyk satiry Saltykova-Shchedrina* (Moscow: Moskovskii universitet, 1953).

9. Where Porfirii's language mocks Russian traditionalism, Stepan's is a bizarre mélange of Gallicisms, pompous literary expressions, coarse collo-

quialisms, and even Church Slavonicisms, reflecting the cultural chaos resulting from an unassimilated Westernization.

10. "Psycho-Analytic Notes on an Autobiographical Account of a Case of Paranoia (Dementia Paranoides)" (1911), *The Standard Edition of the Complete Psychological Works of Sigmund Freud*, ed. and trans. James Strachey (London: Hogarth, 1953–), 12:70–71.

11. Stepan goes home as if to "The Last Judgment," where he will receive "retribution" for his wasted life (29–30).

12. Saltykov, though not a believer, traced the origins of his thirst for social justice and individual freedom to his boyhood reading of the Evangels – a testimony not uncommon among Russian radicals of his age. See *Poshekhonskaia starina, Sobranie sochinenii* (1965–75), 17:68–71.

13. See Balukhatyi, *Russkie pisateli o literature*, 2:249.

14. *Sochineniia i pis'ma* (Moscow: A. I. Mamontov, 1913–14), 1:79.

15. Quoted by Franco Venturi, *Roots of Revolution*, trans. Francis Haskell (New York: Knopf, 1964), 34.

16. V. G. Belinskii, "Literaturnye mechtaniia," *Sobranie sochinenii* (Moscow: Khudozhestvennaia literatura, 1948), 1:7–9 and passim. D. S. Merezhkovskii, "O prichinakh upadka i o novykh techeniiakh sovremennoi russkoi literatury," *Izbrannye stat'i* (Munich: Wilhelm Fink, 1972), 209–20.

Satiric Form in Saltykov's
Gospoda Golovlevy

KARL D. KRAMER

We no longer associate satire with a specific literary form, but rather with a writer's attitude toward his material. Northrop Frye, for example, justifiably describes satire, together with tragedy, comedy, romance, and irony, as a category prior to genre, because these "mythoi" or "generic plots" cut across the conception of literary form;[1] thus satire, or any other mythos, may be embodied in various forms, such as the drama, novel, or narrative poem. Nevertheless, distinct formal consequences arise out of the special problem facing the satirist: He specifically sets out to represent a world dominated by absurd behavior and irrational undertakings that result in self-destruction; he places before his readers a vision of the world in chaos, though he does this ordinarily from a stable, reasonable, and morally healthy point of view. In this way satire exposes what the author takes to be vice or folly in terms of its absurdity; irony and wit are its characteristic devices. But the exposure itself results in a conflict between the madness the satirist depicts and the reasonable perspective through which the chaotic is labeled as such. In this respect we must distinguish between satire and what Frye calls irony, particularly modern works that reflect chaos without the satirist's reasonable perspective (Kafka's grotesques or Camus' *The Stranger*, for example).

The special problem of the satirist, then, is to embody his vision of chaos within a literary form. But form is a way of ordering experience, of organizing meaning, while the satirist endeavors to represent experience that tends constantly to become ever more chaotic and ever less meaningful. We make generic divisions on the basis of form, and yet the very notion of form is alien to the material of satire. Because of this, the question of genre in satire has always been a thorny one. The satirist is compelled to work within literary types for which his material is necessarily ill-adapted. The nineteenth-century novel, for instance, normally records the gradual rise of the hero's fortunes, or at least offers a satisfactory resolution of the problems the novel poses; it leads from failure to success, or darkness to clarity. In this sense its general shape might be represented by an ascending line. But the general pattern in satire would have to be represented by a descending one, for the intent is to expose the foolishness or absurdity of its protagonists. Thus the satirist writing novels in the nineteenth century necessarily undermines the accepted form. As Robert C. Elliott has observed, there has traditionally been a sense of disorderliness in satire that can be traced back to classical literature: Roman satire has its origins in a motley collection of Greek forms.[2] This impression of a hodgepodge may directly reflect the incompatibility between satire and any literary form, which is a persistent problem. Alvin B. Kernan has noted the disparity between the neatness, evenness, and balance of Dryden's heroic couplets and the freaks who are pinioned by the form in *Absalom and Acitophel*.[3] At least one satirist, Saltykov-Shchedrin, solved this problem by claiming he could disregard the demands of form; he may have reflected an attitude typical of the satirist when he made this comment on his own book, *Istoriia odnogo goroda*:

> The history book form of the story gave me certain advantages, as did the form of a story told by an archivist. But in essence I have never been put under a restraint by form and have used it only insofar as I have found it necessary. In one place I would speak in the person of the archivist, in another in my own; in one place I would confine myself to the historical evidence, in another I would talk of facts which at the given time did not exist. And it seems to me that in view of the purposes toward which I strive, such a free attitude toward form is quite permissible.[4]

More frequently, however, the incongruity of means and ends has erupted in parody, the most basic satiric form. Parody involves the replacement of the conventional by the ridiculous, when the author assumes a playful attitude, and by the odious when he assumes a grim one. The degrees between the ridiculous and the odious would include such categories as the absurd, the grotesque, and the monstrous. At one extreme, Cervantes substitutes windmills for giants; at the other, Swift in *A Modest Proposal* substitutes the abhorrent for the practicable: he suggests we solve the Irish population problem by eating the excess babies.

The tendency in satire, then, is toward a negation of whatever conventional form the satirist chooses to work in, and this may well be why parody is nearly always associated with it. When satiric intent and formal demands are operating at cross purposes, the artistic confrontation is likely to result in parody, but at less critical moments the satirist will casually disregard those conventions that do not serve his purposes. If we are to grasp the form of any satiric work, we must view it in relation to the conventions of the genre in which it purports to have been written.

Saltykov's best known work, *Gospoda Golovlyovy*, represents an interesting test case because it is not ordinarily considered a satire at all, but rather a fairly conventional, if searingly critical, social novel. It deals with a distinct, historically recognizable social group in Russia – the provincial gentry of the nineteenth century, the same group Goncharov had represented earlier in *Oblomov*. In form it bears at least a superficial resemblance to the novel that deals with the history of a family (Aksakov's *Semeinaia khronika* [Family chronicle], for example). Unquestionably, the book puts to its own uses a number of conventions of the nineteenth-century realistic novel, and this is perhaps why many critics call it a representative specimen of that type. But its form will come into better focus if we postulate that it is a satire in novelistic dress and if we then proceed to examine how Saltykov manipulates our expectations within this form. I believe it can be shown that, because he was first and foremost a satirist, he ultimately produced a work that parodies the family novel and either ignores or violates most of the novelistic conventions of his day. In this respect, the problem of identifying the form of *Gospoda Golovlyovy* resembles similar difficulties encountered in the study of *Gulliver's Travels*, another satire that employs elements, at least, of novelistic convention. It might be said that *Gospoda Golovlyovy* is contiguous with the nineteenth-century Russian novel, though not a representative member of the group, just as *Gulliver's Travels* is contiguous with the eighteenth-century English novel. However, *Gospoda Golovlyovy* offers an additional complication in the relationship between the reader's expectations and satiric form; this relationship happens to be a two-way street: Saltykov the satirist does transform novelistic conventions, but the pressure of the novel genre alters the identity of several satiric devices as well – a process that further muddies the formal outlines of the work.

Before we examine the effects of satire on the novel, it may be useful to uncover some typical satiric devices that lie embedded in the texture of Saltykov's book. In his discussion of *Timon of Athens* Elliott notes the dominant role played by the "conventional wit-combat in invective" of satire.[5] Actually, *Gospoda Golovlyovy* contains a classic instance of this in the vituperative exchanges between Arina Petrovna and her husband Vladimir. Elliott also notes that ridicule is one of the primitive functions of satire.[6] The objective stance of the realistic novelist inhibits Saltykov in this regard; but the author is fortuitously relieved of this function by the characters themselves, who liberally bestow libelous nicknames on one another: Arina Petrovna, who has a passion for them, addresses her servant on the opening page as "fickle head" (*suma peremetnaia*); Arina's husband calls his wife "witch" and "devil," while she dubs him "windmill" and "stringless balalaika"; and Stepan has been known from childhood as "boob head" (*balbes*), and as a boy he had bestowed on Porfirii a finished definition of the man in three nicknames, Iudushka (the diminutive form adding insult to injury), "bloodsucker," and "goody-goody" (*otkrovennyi mal'chik*).[7] Saltykov achieves a double victory by this means: the family members effectively identify their respective shortcomings, and at the same time expose their contemptible disdain for one another.

Wit has generally been taken as a characteristic of the satirist, but a sense of the comic appears to be at a premium in *Gospoda Golovlyovy*. Mirsky, who places it squarely in the midst of the Russian realistic tradition, observes: "The book is certainly the gloomiest in all Russian literature."[8] But just because it creates the illusion of stark realism, we tend to overlook the evidence of Saltykov's wit that runs through the entire work. Although Mirsky would seem to place it outside the pale of satire, Northrop Frye has judiciously redefined our conception of satiric wit in a way that clarifies Saltykov's use of it: one of the essential qualities of satire, Frye insists, is "wit or humor founded on fantasy or a sense of the grotesque or absurd."[9] If humor is in relatively short supply, wit founded on "a sense of the grotesque" is certainly omnipresent in *Gospoda Golovlyovy*. A particularly salient example of this is the pattern of self-delusion that we see in Pavel, Arina Petrovna, and Porfirii shortly before their deaths – a delusion that takes the form of grotesque fantasies. Arina's fantasies coincide with the first signs of collapse in her domain – the preparations for the emancipation – when visions of social anarchy dominate her thinking. Pavel, as he gives way to drink, luxuriates in ever more grotesque dreams of triumph over Porfirii:

> Sometimes he would imagine he had won two hundred thousand and he would come to inform Porfishka, whose face would be distorted with envy (a complete scene with dialogue). Sometimes he would imagine that his grandfather had died (again a scene with dialogue, even though he did not have a grandfather), and that he had been left a million, but to Porfishka the bloodsucker absolutely nothing. Sometimes he would imagine that he had invented a way of making himself invisible, and in this form he was able to carry out vicious tricks that would make Porfishka groan. In the invention of these pranks he was inexhaustible and for lengthy periods his nonsensical laughter would fill the upstairs.[10]

At his own end, Porfirii takes delight in such utterly absurd calculations as how much money he could earn from milk if all the cows in the neighborhood except his own were suddenly to die. The continual appearance of such grisly wit throughout the book is surely one sign that we are dealing here with a satiric work.

But the more central issue is the ways in which the satiric intent modifies the conception of the novel. In fact, *Gospoda Golovlyovy* was not initially intended to be a novel, but rather another series of sketches dealing with the landowner, to be published in turn as they were written in *Otechestvennye zapiski* [Notes of the Fatherland]. After the appearance of the first sketch in 1875 Turgenev wrote Saltykov suggesting that instead of sketches this account of provincial life might well be turned into a full-blown novel.[11] Despite his apparent acceptance of Turgenev's advice, Saltykov was clearly unsympathetic to the treatment of life in the contemporary novel.[12] In an earlier work, *Gospoda Tashkenttsy* [The Gentlemen of Tashkent], he had declared himself dissatisfied with the novel that is orientated toward the family and in which the intrigue turns on love: "It seems to me that the novel has lost its former basis, since the family and everything connected with it has begun to change its character. The novel (at least in the way it has appeared till now) is chiefly a work about family life. Its drama begins in the family, does not go outside it, and ends there, too. Whether in a positive sense (the English novel) or in a negative one (the French novel), family life plays the central role in the novel."[13] Aware of Saltykov's conviction that the family novel had become outmoded, a recent Soviet critic, Kamsar Grigor'ian, has quite reasonably asked why this satirist should write a family novel himself some five years later.[14] Grigor'ian's answer, that this is only a superficial impression and that the real heart of the work is a sociological study, simply ignores most of the book's content; *Gospoda Golovlyovy* does concentrate on a study of family life. The more obvious answer is that Saltykov did what satirists ordinarily do: he wrote a parody – in this instance a parody of the conventional, family-oriented novel.

Arina Petrovna Golovlyova, the mother, exhibits one aspect of this parody when she turns the idea of the family into the chief source of her own hypocrisy: "Under these circumstances Arina Petrovna had early felt isolated so that actually she became completely unaccustomed even to family life, although the word *family* never left her tongue, and ostensibly, incessant anxiety about the arrangement of family affairs was the sole guide in all her actions" (104–5; *SS*, 13:9–10). Saltykov shows another aspect of this parody when he portrays Ulita, a Golovlyov servant, as a caricature of the faithful old family retainer. Like the Golovlyovs themselves, she has spent a lifetime trying to attain power by any means, but she is left at the end with nothing more than gratifying memories of enemas she has administered to three generations of the family.

A striking collection of metaphors centers on the business of feeding. In these situations nature is turned upside down so that the mother figuratively devours her own children. The eldest son, Stepan, returning home to die in the opening chapter, predicts that his mother will gobble him up (*zaest ona menia*).[15] When Stepan confronts his father shortly afterward, Vladimir Golovlyov shouts, "'She'll eat you up, eat you up, eat you up!'" (*s"est! s"est! s"est!*). Confined to a single room in the family home and put on a starvation diet by Arina Petrovna, Stepan finds he can think only of food. Arina is eventually forced to admit that she cannot actually allow her son to starve to death, but the realization that she must keep him alive is a depressing one for her. When Arina contemplates the disaster of the liberation of the serfs, she characteristically worries about the servants' eating wastefully. Even Porfirii Golovlyov's nickname, "bloodsucker," has a grotesque relevance in the context of feeding imagery.

A theme closely related to the parody of the family, and particularly to the feeding imagery, is Saltykov's play on the parable of the prodigal son. He takes its central idea – "for this my son was dead, and is alive again; he was lost and is found" (Luke, 15:24) – and reverses the conception, so that the prodigal son invariably encounters his death when he returns home. Stepan thinks of the parable as he approaches the family estate but realizes that for him the equation is merely a delusion. Nevertheless, while starving in his room, he dreams of feasting on the fatted calf, a point where the feeding imagery and the parable clearly meet. Like Stepan, Annin'ka, a Golovlyov niece, returns to the family homestead for the sole purpose of dying. Porfirii Golovlyov's son, Petia, returns home a ruined man to beg money from his father, who refuses him any assistance, thus forcing Petia to Siberian exile and death. Porfirii goes one step further in the corruption of the parable when he takes it upon himself to send his illegitimate baby away to an orphanage in Moscow. But he ultimately reverts to the role of son himself in the book's final scene, when he goes out to die at the foot of his mother's grave.

Such a treatment of family life contrasts sharply with that presented in any representative nineteenth-century novel. In *David Copperfield*, for example, the family unit clearly signifies a normal and desirable basis for happiness. Most of its family groups lack one or more essential members, and this lack is usually associated with their problems: Steerforth explicitly attributes his wayward nature to the absence of a father in his youth; Uriah Heep also lacks a father, as does David, who is given a travesty of one in Murdstone; Mr. Wickfield's wife has died, and he attributes the unhealthy atmosphere of the Wickfield home to this; the Peggottys are a family group that consists of miscellaneous relatives. In fact, the only wholly normal family unit in the entire book is the Micawbers, and their attraction is closely connected with this normality. As the Micawber–Heep relationship rises to a crisis, Mrs. Micawber defines the change in her husband in terms of his sudden alienation from his family. David's final triumph over his experience is represented by a happy marriage and a plethora of children. Clearly, in regard to the family, Saltykov is parodying a convention that Dickens wholeheartedly embraced.

Saltykov either ignores or corrupts the romantic interests so characteristic of the novel generally. We have here an area in which the satirist can largely ignore a novelistic convention. In the case of Arina Petrovna, he goes out of his way to emphasize the absence of romantic love. She objects to her husband's affairs with the servants not because she is jealous, but rather because she fears this may undermine her authority in the household. Saltykov reverses the roles of husband and wife when he explains that Arina, disappointed in domestic life, seeks refuge in her financial enterprises. In fact, romance has impinged on her experience only through the joy she feels in spying out the maids' amours.

Saltykov follows somewhat the same procedure in regard to Porfirii; no conventional novel representing the history of a family could possibly neglect the central character's wife as *Gospoda Golovlyovy* does. Porfirii's mate is apparently alive during the period described in the second chapter, but she is long dead by the beginning of the third. Actually she never appears in the book. However, the pull of the novel forces Saltykov to deal with his hero's romantic side in some fashion, and the natural resolution is parody, or at least the total corruption of romantic yearnings. Instead of a wife, what we actually observe are his illicit affair with the housemaid Evpraksiia and his amorous interest in his niece Annin'ka. In both instances the satirical intent is particularly strong. Describing Porfirii's interest in Annin'ka, Saltykov writes: "Iudushka loved his God more than anything, but this did not prevent him from having a taste for beautiful women, especially if they were tall. Therefore, he first made the sign of the cross over Annin'ka, then somehow particularly pointedly kissed her on both cheeks and, as he did this, peered so oddly at her bust that Annin'ka could not entirely hide a smile" (180; *SS*, 13:142). Thus Saltykov ignores the romantic element wherever possible and parodies it with respect to his hero.

Dramatic conflict lies at the basis of plot in the nineteenth-century novel. The conflict depends on the reader's willingness to accept the existence of opposing interests or convictions and, further, to sympathize with and be hostile to the appropriate sides in these oppositions. But in satire the reader is seldom asked to suspend his disbelief in this way. Perhaps this is an inevitable consequence of parody – of substituting the ridiculous for the conventional. The terms of the conflict are ordinarily so dependent on abstract conceptions that the dramatic conflict vanishes before the practical absurdity of the world depicted; men become Lilliputians or Brobdingnagians or philosophers like Dr. Pangloss. To the extent that *Don*

Quixote is a satire parodying chivalric romances it could be argued that nothing happens when the hero sallies forth in search of adventure; the dramatic conflict of chivalric romance vanishes because of the absence of any antagonist more formidable than a windmill or a flock of sheep. In *Gospoda Golovlyovy* the natural source of dramatic conflict similarly collapses. If the book were a social novel, then the most likely source of conflict would be that between the chief representative of the decaying provincial gentry and those whom he exploits and oppresses. But Saltykov reduces his villain to the proportions of a bore. He is simply a menace to be avoided:

> Iudushka was not liked. Not that it was impossible to get around him, but he was extremely fond of triviality and would bore and pester a person. Few people would venture even to rent a plot of land from him, because he would give the plot and then for every extra inch ploughed or mowed, for every minute of overdue rent, he would immediately start dragging the tenant through the courts. He did this to many people and ruined them through red tape and idleness, though he himself won nothing; his habit of quibbling was known everywhere, so that his claim would be dismissed with the barest examination of the case. (148; *SS*, 13:86)

Indeed, this description of Porfirii's relations with his neighbors is the closest the book comes to representing social conflict. For the most part social relationships exist only within the Golovlyov family itself. The most dramatic scene in the entire work is the one in which Arina Petrovna lays a curse on her son, Porfirii, and yet even here the author deliberately smothers a good deal of the dramatic impact: although Arina has been toying for years with the idea of the curse, and though Porfirii has long dreaded it, he is indifferent when it actually happens; he had imagined a scene rampant with superstitious signs of God's immediate vengeance, but when she does finally curse him in broad daylight, he is left unperturbed. Pofirii himself contains no surprises; his nature is summed up in his nicknames at the beginning of the book, and he is nothing if not consistent.

Indeed, one of Saltykov's chief problems in writing the book must have been the avoidance of tediousness, for it certainly exhibits very little drama. It consists largely of narrative by omniscient author, and scenes of confrontation between characters are the exception. Instead, Saltykov's narrative voice expresses an intellectual orientation which, again, is the hallmark of the satirist. In a wasteland of vileness the reader's only contact with a morally healthy voice comes by way of the narrator, who establishes a sorely needed screen between the action and the reader's perception of it. Without this intervening agent the work would probably belong to what Northrop Frye calls the ironic mythos, rather than the satiric, for the reader would then have no basis for a reasonable perspective from which to view the Golovlyov madness. This voice, which constantly interrupts the narrative proper, exhibits three distinct attitudes toward the action: ironic, critical, and analytic. We hear the ironic voice describing Arina Petrovna's reaction to her husband's last words; Vladimir has just expressed his relief in knowing that he will die before the emancipation of the serfs, and thus avoid the necessity of appearing arm in arm with them before his Maker: "These words were deeply impressed on the sensitive soul of Arina Petrovna" (133; SS, 13:59). We hear the critical voice in this comment on Arina's attitude toward Stepan: "She completely lost sight of the fact that near her in the office there lived a being connected to her by blood ties, a being who might be yearning for life" (128; SS, 13:50). Examples of the analytic voice are generally too long to quote here; suffice it to mention the digression where the author compares Porfirii's hypocrisy with Tartuffe's (ch. 3).

If Saltykov holds dramatic conflict to a minimum, he is virtually forced to construct his plot in a way that makes it a travesty of itself – a consequence that, as satirist, he readily accepts. Each chapter emerges as a separate entity dealing with a particular character, and most of the chapters are resolved by the death of that character. It is important to dwell for a moment on the action depicted in each episode with this point in mind.

Chapter 1 centers on Stepan's return home and his death. Chapter 2 describes the death of another son, Pavel. Chapter 3 involves Porfirii's son Petia, whom Porfirii abandons. Chapter 4 relates Arina Petrovna's death and introduces a new character, Annin'ka, who promptly departs at the end of the chapter. Chapters 5 and 6 detail Porfirii's relation with Evpraksiia; chapter 5 culminates in his abandoning his baby, chapter 6 in the servant's domination of the master. And, finally, chapter 7 describes the return of Annin'ka, who dies together with Porfirii.

All this means that the characters have little opportunity to interact. With the exception of Porfirii, who does manage to hold out to the end of the book, and Arina Petrovna, who survives at least the first half, the characters appear merely for the purpose of disappearing or dying. The dominant event throughout the book, then, is a series of deaths – an anti-event that is clearly related to the negation of plot interest.

The grotesque monotony of the plot is underlined in other ways as well: the story moves from Stepan's drunken fantasies in chapter 1 to Porfirii's drunken fantasies at the very end of the book. As Pavel is dying, Porfirii hovers in the background, waiting to absorb the family estate, just as in the final lines, when Porfirii lies frozen at the foot of his mother's grave, "a new rider was dispatched and sent to Goriushkino to 'little sister' Nadezhda Ivanovna Galkina (Aunt Varvara Mikhailovna's daughter), who, ever since last autumn, had kept a vigilant eye on everything that occurred at Golovlyovo" (248; *SS*, 13:262). Annin'ka's appearance more than halfway through the story further increases the vile monotony of the experience depicted throughout the book; though she comes from the world beyond the Golovlyov estate and though it is only in the description of her experience that we move outside the bounds of the household, nevertheless her history repeats the same motifs: the suicide of her sister, the death of her lover, and stupefying drunkenness.

Alvin B. Kernan has noted a general pattern operative in satire whereby an apparent rise in the hero's fortunes inevitably presages his ultimate downfall. In connection with plot, he observes that it will of necessity appear "disjunct":

Dullness drives toward a dismemberment of form and this drive is manifested – consistently – on all levels of the plot. But we have also noted a complex, ironic quality in the movements of dullness: it strives in spite of nature to create Progress yet always produces its opposite. The rise becomes a fall, the advance a circular wandering, the brave new world a living hell; the search for the philosophers' stone eats up the wealth it was intended to produce; the dunce who sets up for a wit only succeeds in making his weaknesses apparent. In satire we are shown that it is the very nature of dullness to defeat itself, even when it *appears* to succeed, believes it has succeeded.[16]

This statement ideally formulates the process through which both Arina Petrovna and Porfirii pass in the course of *Gospoda Golovlyovy*. Each in turn is ever more successful in acquiring wealth, and inevitably the higher each rises the greater the ultimate downfall. The instrument of their downfall is hypocrisy, which is also a major theme in *David Copperfield*; there are instructive differences between the two books in this regard, as well as in their treatment of the family. In *David Copperfield* deception serves a purpose – both Murdstone and Uriah Heep seek power, Steerforth wishes to seduce Emily, and so on. In addition, the villains are ultimately exposed by forces outside themselves, just as their deceptions have been outwardly directed. But in *Gospoda Golovlyovy* hypocrisy becomes the chief element in that self-deception which finally destroys everyone.

In the context of satire, then, we may say that hypocrisy in the latter work has no goal at all; the characters are zealously engaged in eliminating themselves from the book. They are, interestingly, a nearly self-contained unit within it. As has been pointed out, the reader sees them almost exclusively in their relations with one another, and finally they become their own judges and executioners, the latter primarily by means of alcohol.

The process of self-deception through hypocrisy is clear in Arina Petrovna: "All her life she had been establishing something, had wasted away for something, now it appeared she had been wasting away over a phantom. Throughout her life the word *family* had never deserted her tongue; in the name of the family she had punished some and rewarded others; in the name of the family she had subjected herself to privations, had tormented herself, crippled her whole life – and what if it should turn out that a family was precisely what she did not have!" (138; *SS*, 13:68). Porfirii is often considered a fairly sly rogue who succeeds in concentrating the family wealth in his own hands, defeating even Arina Petrovna, the architect of this fortune. Actually he is nothing of the sort; it is the waning of Arina's faculties, rather than any brilliance on Porfirii's part that accounts for the collapse of her powers. This is clear in the early part of the book where Saltykov describes how Arina was bewildered by Porfirii as a child, although his brother had even then read his character sufficiently well to bestow the familiar nicknames on him.

The matter of Porfirii's self-destruction, especially at the very end, is rather more problematic. There is a definite, if limited, awareness on his part that his life has been miserably and senselessly wasted when he reflects on Christ's death: "'Ah, what sufferings those were! It's only through such sufferings that a person can . . . And He forgave! forgave everyone and forever! He forgave everyone! not only those who then gave Him vinegar with gall to drink, but also those who later, even now, and in the future forever and ever will bring to his lips vinegar mingled with gall. . . . Horrible! Ah, it's horrible!" (248; *SS*, 13:261). Later the same night Porfirii walks out of the house into a blizzard, thereby virtually committing suicide. This final scene was written several years after Goncharov had zealously endeavored to instruct Saltykov on what he should not do with his hero:

> He can never turn out well, as you will see yourself when you get to the end. He can change in any way you wish; that is, you can make him worse and worse: he can lose everything he's gained, move to a hut with no chimney for its fireplace, endure all humiliations, die on a dunghill, like an old galosh that has been thrown away, but to rise inwardly – no, no, and no! . . . Actually to inflict

a wound on oneself with a knife, to put a bullet through the forehead – this means, at any rate, to be aware of some kind of horror at one's position, to be aware of the despair of collapse; it means feeling that one does have some guts, but this is not the case with such a nature – he neither has sufficient strength for this nor is the material at all present! Only being afraid could force him to make such an attempt.[17]

In view of both Turgenev and Goncharov having made suggestions for the final shape of the work, Saltykov had quite a formidable battery of literary counselors, whose advice he quietly rejected. He did not produce the "full-blown novel" Turgenev had recommended nor did he reject the notion of Porfirii's suicide, as Goncharov had proposed. In fact Porfirii obviously does experience horror in contemplating his position, and it is certainly not fear that prompts him to take his own life. It is, rather, his sense of total confusion. His moral qualms after the Easter service indicate one aspect of this confusion. When these feelings are immediately juxtaposed with his conviction that he has betrayed his mother, of all people, we begin to sense the chaos of feeling in which he has become embroiled, for in one way this conviction is quite accurate: In his ultimate collapse he has betrayed the inspiration for his own hypocrisy and the source of his power. His decision to throw himself on his mother's grave is, then, a consummate, and therefore utterly meaningless, gesture in the sense that he is disgusted by his hypocrisy *and* by his betrayal of the principle of hypocrisy itself. In his discussion of Porfirii's state during the last hours, Saltykov analyzes his central character in just such terms: "And only now, when Annin'ka had awakened in him an awareness of the 'desolation' he had wrought, did he understand for the first time that this tale [the crucifixion of Christ] was about an unheard-of falsehood that a sanguinary injustice had carried out against truth. . . . Of course it would be an exaggeration to say that by virtue of this discovery any kind of vital confrontation had arisen in his soul, but there is no doubt that a confusion almost verging on despair had formed in it" (247; SS, 13:260).

Saltykov could have resolved Porfirii's fate in one of several ways. At one extreme he might have tried to redeem him, but this would have been utterly inconsistent with the tenor of the rest of the book; at the other extreme he could have allowed him simply to drink himself to death, as Stepan had done. Although this might have been consistent, Porfirii, as the arch exponent of the family vices, deserves something more overwhelming. What Saltykov actually does is to combine the two extremes and thereby produce in Porfirii an ultimate bewilderment that goes beyond the desolation which had overtaken his relatives. There is, as well, an important element of parody in Porfirii's decision to throw his life away during Easter week in a mood of religious fervor; the exultation of eternal life that the Easter ceremony symbolizes inspires Porfirii's ultimate destruction.

Gospoda Golovlyovy is, then, a satiric work, exposing the absurdity and madness to which the protagonists' hypocrisy leads them. In writing the book Saltykov created a parody of the novel form as he knew it – in particular, a parody of the novel that focuses on family life. Admittedly his form veers toward the grim extreme – the mother devouring her offspring, the father rejecting the prodigal son, the uncle making love to his niece, a man committing suicide under the inspiration of the Easter ceremony – but a pattern certainly does emerge in which he substitutes the odious for the conventional. Moreover, the abatement of dramatic conflict reduces the plot to a series of fragmentary episodes devoted to the dissolution of a whole cast of characters. Thus material that in the hands of a novelist might have produced a social novel becomes, in the satirist's hands, a caricature of the novel form itself; Saltykov successfully subverted the conventions of the genre to his own satiric purposes.

NOTES

1. Northrop Frye, *Anatomy of Criticism* (Princeton, N.J.: Princeton University Press, 1957), 162.

2. Robert C. Elliott, *The Power of Satire: Magic, Ritual, Art* (Princeton, N.J.: Princeton University Press, 1960), 104–5.

3. Alvin B. Kernan, *The Plot of Satire* (New Haven, Conn.: Yale University Press, 1965), 17–18.

4. M. E. *Saltykov-Shchedrin o literature i iskusstve*, ed. L. F. Ershov (Moscow: Iskusstvo, 1953), 405.

5. Elliott, *The Power of Satire*, 159.

6. Ibid., 66–87.

7. Andrew R. MacAndrew gives this version of *otkrovennyi mal'chik* in his translation of *The Golovlovs* (New York: New American Library, 1961).

8. D. S. Mirsky, *A History of Russian Literature*, ed. Francis J. Whitfield (New York: Knopf, 1949), 281.

9. Frye, *Anatomy of Criticism*, 224.

10. M. E. Saltykov-Shchedrin, "Gospoda Golovlyovy," *Izbrannye sochineniia*, ed. A. Lavretskii (Moscow-Leningrad: Goslitizdat, 1947), 137. Further quotations from this work are cited by page number within the text. [References to *Sobranie sochinenii* (1965–77) have been added by me. – ED.]

11. See Turgenev's letter of 28 October 1875 in M. S. Goriachkina, ed., *M. E. Saltykov-Shchedrin v russkoi kritike* (Moscow: Khudozhestvennaia literatura, 1959), 580–81.

12. See, particularly, his satirical review of a work by A. K. Tolstoi in *Saltykov o literature*, 64–65.

13. M. E. Saltykov-Shchedrin, *Sobranie sochinenii* (Moscow: Pravda, 1951), 5:29–30.

14. K. N. Grigor'ian, *Roman M. E. Saltykova-Shchedrina "Gospoda Golovlyovy"* (Moscow-Leningrad: Akademiia nauk, 1962), 25.

15. The Russian word *zaest'* is used here to mean "to worry a person to death"; however, this is clearly a metaphorical extension of its basic meaning, "to take a bite."

16. Kernan, *The Plot of Satire*, 102.

17. Letter of 30 December 1876 from Goncharov in Goriachkina, *Saltykov-Shchedrin v russkoi kritike*, 586–87.

Satirical Elements in *The Golovlyovs*

I. P. FOOTE

When publication of *The Golovlyovs* began, contemporary critics noted that Saltykov was changing course, abandoning his role of satirist for that of "artist." It was a generally valid observation, for *The Golovlyovs* was distinctly different from his run-of-the mill satirical sketches. However, in the novel as a whole there are signs enough of Saltykov's irrepressible satirical verve to remind the reader of the author's main métier. Some of the satire occurs in brief passing references, the significance of which might elude the casual reader. In "Family Court," for instance, when Porfirii hears of Stepan's misdemeanors, he "was ready to rend his garments, but feared that here in the country there might be nobody to mend them" – a bathetic juxtaposition of biblical reference (rending clothes in anger or grief) and mundane consideration that might seem just a joke, but in fact is a succinct satirical characterization of Porfirii, who combines ostentatious piety with material calculation. Another brief, satirically loaded remark is Evpraksiia's reply when Annin'ka asks if she is not bored in Golovlyovo: "What call is there to be bored, Miss? We're not gentry" – boredom, she recognizes, is a prerogative of the leisured class.

Most of the satire is more overt and is directed at the various social types who came regularly under Saltykov's fire. Familiar targets in his sketches, apart from the declining gentry, were government officials and the ways of bureaucracy, lawyers (newly emerged as a profession), bourgeois entrepreneurs, and the zemstvos (local government organs introduced in the 1860s). All these, satirically presented, find a place in *The Golovlyovs*, for the most part in those sections of the novel relating to Annin'ka and Liubin'ka in their theatrical peregrinations through the provinces.

Bureaucrats and bureaucratism are touched on more than once. Porfirii, with his "thirty years" of service as a government official, dismays Arina Petrovna with the petty accounting he demands from her for the produce of Golovlyovo; his experience of futile bureaucratic procedures ("pouring from the empty into the void" [*perelivat' iz pustogo v porozhnoe*]) inspires him to follow the same practices on his estate, where he fills his time with recording useless information and making pointless calculations. (Saltykov even throws in a bureaucratic joke about the official who calculated the national potato yield by dividing a map of the empire into squares, then multiplying the number of squares by a potatoes-per-acre figure obtained from a greengrocer; the answer was meaningless, but bureaucratic form was satisfied.) More serious aspects of officialdom – its corruption and coercion – are referred to in episodes from the twins' career as provincial actresses. There is the police chief of Samovarnov who harasses them with petty official impingements when their hospitality falls below the level appropriate to his station, and who initiates proceedings against Annin'ka's "protector," Kukishev, when the latter rashly refuses to make him a "loan" (i.e., submit to extortion). Kukishev and Liul'kin (a zemstvo official and Liubin'ka's lover) are both members of the Samovarnov Town Council and no less corrupt than officials of the central government; their downfall comes when they are exposed as embezzlers. In the late 1870s, when the novel was written, the authorities were on the defensive against revolutionaries and took restrictive measures to curb the spread of their influence: passing references are made to this – for instance, in the episode of Annin'ka's complaining of Kukishev's harassment to the "head of the district" (*nachal'nik kraia*, i.e., "governor of the province") who has "expended all his strength in the conflict with internal enemies [i.e., revolutionary agitators]," and in Porfirii's joking (?) statements, when conversing with the priest in "Illicit Family Joys," that eating and drinking are *not* forbidden by the government ("eat by all means – as long as you keep a bridle on your tongue") and that birds enjoy unrestrained freedom and are not answerable "to God or to the authorities." In a similar vein, in "Kith and Kin" he fends off

Arina Petrovna's request for a turkey from Golovlyovo by declaring that all the turkeys had died (in neglect of their duty to feed their masters) – "so typical in this present age of freedom." The authorities' fear of public demonstrations is touched on in Petenka's reference to the funeral of the operetta artiste Liadova – "two thousand people followed her coffin . . . they thought there was going to be a revolution." Ironies of this kind may be found in any of Saltykov's satirical sketches.

A satirical note is present also in the portrayal of representatives of the legal and medical professions and of the clergy, who appear episodically in the novel. Lawyers, who took on a public role when open court proceedings were introduced in the 1860s, early established a dubious reputation for their arrogant pretensions and legal manipulations. Among their detractors were Tolstoy (in *Anna Karenina*) and Dostoevsky (in *The Brothers Karamazov*), and Saltykov weighs in, in *The Golovlyovs*, with Pavel's skeptical view of lawyers as predatory birds ("once a lawyer gets wind of it that you've got property, he'll start hovering for the kill") and Annin'ka's account of the frivolities of her lawyer friends, who pass forged banknotes (!) – later the sisters suffer humiliation in court from the exhibitionist prosecutor who plays to the gallery. There is one doctor (in "Kith and Kin") – a *bon viveur* who decries modern medicine, declares Pavel's case as hopeless, and shows more interest in the refreshments available than in his patient. The clergy who show up at Golovlyov occasions (Pavel's funeral, Evpraksiia's confinement) are cast by Saltykov in their traditional role as prodigious eaters and drinkers, as well as subservient dependents of the local gentry, who, besides providing them with opportunities to gormandize, are a source of funds for parish needs – not for nothing does the priest summoned to Evpraksiia choose to regard Porfirii's heterodox views not as blasphemy but as merely "the natural audacity of mind to be expected from the gentry class."

The new bourgeois entrepreneur, familiar in *Well-Intentioned Speeches* (Derunov), *The Refuge of Mon Repos* (Razuvaev), and other sketches of the 1870s, is represented in *The Golovlyovs* by the brash, uneducated Kukishev, one-time small trader, now a "purveyor of high-class drapery" and prosperous enough to compete in fast living with the "retired captain of hussars" Liul'kin. Pitiful though the outcome is for Annin'ka, his crude "courtship" of her has its comic-satirical aspect. Characteristically Kukishev accepts his downfall with primitive resignation – he has yet to attain the refinement of the gentry-born Liul'kin, who, when his peculation is discovered, "honorably" blows his brains out.

Insignificant though these satirical elements may be relative to the main theme of *The Golovlyovs*, their presence in the novel is a clear enough sign of the author's attachment to his customary mode of writing. And they do something, too, to lighten the prevailing gloom of the narrative.

III  PRIMARY SOURCES

Letters

The following extracts from letters of Saltykov (letters 1–7) relate to the writing of *The Golovlyovs* up to the chapter "Escheated." Regrettably, his extant correspondence contains no reference to the composition of the final chapter ("The Reckoning"). Letters to him containing favorable comment on the novel as it was being written (two, at least, from Nekrasov, to which Saltykov refers in replying, as well as letters from others, including probably P. V. Annenkov) have also not survived. There are, though, important letters from Turgenev, A. M. Zhemchuzhnikov, and Goncharov (letters 8–11) in which they express their views on the novel and how it might develop. The encouragement and advice of Turgenev and Zhemchuzhnikov undoubtedly had some influence on the composition of the work; Turgenev's suggestion that Saltykov should write a full-scale novel and Zhemchuzhnikov's proposal for a more detailed account of Porfirii's relationship with Evpraksiia were both taken up by Saltykov. Goncharov's letter, written before "The Reckoning" was begun, concerns the problem of how to bring Judas to a suitable end; in fact, Saltykov provided a resolution that ran counter to Goncharov's views.

1. SALTYKOV TO N. A. NEKRASOV, 27 SEPTEMBER/ 8 OCTOBER 1875 (FROM PARIS) (*SS*, 18(2): 210)

Yesterday I sent to you . . . at the editorial office [of *NF*] a story, "Family Court." Put it in when you find it convenient. I have got rather fed up with *Well-Intentioned Speeches*, but this year will certainly bring them to an end.

2. SALTYKOV TO N. A. NEKRASOV, 2/14 OCTOBER 1875 (FROM PARIS) (*SS*, 18[2]: 212)

You probably did not like . . . my piece "Family Court." I can see myself that it has come out labored and disjointed, but what can you do? – in general, [when] abroad I do not feel like writing, or find it a strain.

3. SALTYKOV TO N. A. NEKRASOV, 23 OCTOBER/ 4 NOVEMBER 1875 (FROM NICE) (*ss*, 18[2]: 221)

You praise my latest story ["Family Court"] too highly. I personally do not care for it. It strikes me as clumsy and labored. There is no free and easy composition, and I am never satisfied with what is a strain to write.

4. SALTYKOV TO N. A. NEKRASOV, 7/19 JANUARY 1876 (FROM NICE) (*ss*, 18[2]: 248)

By March I will try to send you a separate story in which I will describe the end of the Golovlyov family ["Family Scores," published in *NF*, March 1876]. . . . On my story "Kith and Kin" I am receiving praises from all quarters. Annenkov is enthralled, even Turgenev, who generally prefers to keep quiet, congratulates me. . . . People here have shown me letters from Peter[sburg] telling them to find out if there will not be a sequel. Though it is a stupid question, still it has given me the idea of writing a further story.

5. SALTYKOV TO N. A. NEKRASOV, 6/18 APRIL 1876 (FROM PARIS) (*ss*, 18[2]: 284)

Encouraged by your comments on "Family Scores," today I began to write the end of Judas. I do not yet know if anything will come of it, but if it does you will receive it by 10–12 May Old Style . . . So far I have not plotted the stages of development, but the [basic] theme is that everyone around Judas has died and nobody is willing to live with him because they are *terrified of the dust that fills him*. So he becomes a *person escheated*.

6. SALTYKOV TO N. A. NEKRASOV, 3/15 MAY 1876
(FROM PARIS) (*ss*, 18[2]: 287–88)

I am sending you . . . the end of the story: thank God, I finished it on time and even, in fact, earlier than I had promised. I ask you to change the title: instead of "Escheated" put "Before Escheatment." [The episode was published under this title in *NF*, but in the 1880 separate edition it appeared, substantially revised, as "The Niece." – ED.] In the course of writing, some development of details occurred that prevented me from *finishing* this subject completely. So there will be another new story in August, the final one. It is a pity I put these stories into *Well-Intentioned Speeches*, I should have printed them under a separate heading as "Episodes from the History of a Family." I am actually thinking of publishing them separately under this title in December – it will make 16–17 sheets [i.e., printer's sheets, each of sixteen pages] in the usual format of my works.

7. SALTYKOV TO N. A. NEKRASOV, 9 JULY 1876
(FROM VITENEVO) (*ss*, 19[1]: 9)

[Saltykov informs Nekrasov that he intends sending two pieces for the July or August issues of *NF*, one of which – "the end of Judas" ("Escheated") – he is now writing.]

My only fear is of botching Judas. I have already done half, but it is a muddle and needs to be reshaped and rewritten. This half is difficult because the content is all psychological. The second will be easier.

8. I. S. TURGENEV TO SALTYKOV, 28 OCTOBER/
9 NOVEMBER 1875 (I. S. TURGENEV, *POLNOE
SOBRANIE SOCHINENII I PISEM* [*PSSP*] (MOSCOW-
LENINGRAD, 1960–68); *PIS'MA*, 11:149)

I turn to your latest story in *Notes of the Fatherland*. I received the October number yesterday and, of course, at once read "Family

Court," which I was extremely pleased with. The characters are all powerfully and faithfully drawn: to say nothing of the figure of the mother, who is typical – and has appeared in your works before – she is clearly taken alive – from actual life. But particularly good is the figure of the destitute "Booby" [Stepan Golovlyov] who takes to the bottle. It is so good that one cannot help thinking: why, instead of sketches, does Saltykov not write a large-scale novel with a grouping of characters and events, a guiding idea, and a broad execution? The answer to that might be that others in some degree write novels and novellas, while there is nobody [else] to do what Saltykov does. Anyway, be that as it may, I very much liked "Family Court," and I look forward to further episodes – describing the further achievements of Judas.

9. I. S. TURGENEV TO SALTYKOV, 3/15 JANUARY 1876 (*PSSP; PIS'MA*, 11:190)

I have also read "Kith and Kin" and was very pleased with it: the old woman weeping at sunrise – that is what the French call *une trouvaille*, and her whole person is altogether excellent. To be able to rouse the reader's sympathy for her without softening a single trait in her is something only within the reach of great talents.

10. A. M. ZHEMCHUZHNIKOV TO SALTYKOV, 28 SEPTEMBER 1876 (*LITERATURNOE NASLEDSTVO*, 13–14 [MOSCOW, 1934]; 349)

[A. M. Zhemchuzhnikov was a writer of civic and other verse and one of the trio who created the humorous works of the fictitious "Koz'ma Prutkov." He was a close associate of the Nekrasov circle.]

I am very pleased with your "Escheated." Let me tell you that I am absolutely delighted with your Judas. He is, in my opinion, one of your very best creations. This character is totally alive. It is subtly conceived, but firmly and boldly executed. The result is an unusually typical personality. I find it most interesting. In it there is a wonderfully artistic combination of almost ludicrous comedy and profound tragedy. And these two elements, seemingly opposite, are in him indivisible. You would like to go on laughing, but, no, you cannot; it is awful even to laugh; he is terrifying. Nor can you react to him with moral indignation and anger, because he is indisputably comic, particularly when he does what he considers to be the most important thing morally: when he discourses about God or prays to Him with upraised hands. I was sorry that you did not give a more detailed description of the scenes of Evpraksiia's confinement. I picture Judas at this time awaiting with equal submission the will of Providence – either a happy or an unhappy outcome of the birth. He is only concerned by the fact that it will be a long time before the result is known, and several times he sets to upraising his hands. I mention this not as "criticism," but because I find Judas very interesting and would like to see more of him alive. After all, death is now already approaching him. His end, too, greatly interests me. I do not know how you yourself regard Judas or what comments you have heard on this character you have created. For me he is one of your very best creations.

I I. I. A. GONCHAROV TO SALTYKOV, 30 DECEMBER 1876
(I. A. GONCHAROV, *SOBRANIE SOCHINENII* [MOSCOW,
1952–55], 8:489–91)

Allow me to say a further word or two to you on the subject of your character Judas: it is very much on my mind – but then I hardly ever have occasion to talk of these things – because of old age and because I have no one to talk [about them] to.

. . . You are right in saying that he must have his *Sedan* [The Prussian defeat of the French army under Emperor Napoleon III in September 1870, which led to Napoleon's downfall – ED.] a Sedan precisely, only in the sense of an end. The actual hero of Sedan (i.e., Napoleon), a man also of no inner substance, did not charge forward to face the bullets and the bayonets (as did one of his generals – Douay, I think) when he saw that it was all over; instead he lay down his sword at the feet of Wilhelm and lit a cigarette. In Wilhelmshöhe [where Napoleon was held prisoner – ED.] he went skating, and he met his downfall only from a rupture of the bladder.

Your Judas might be struck by a thunderbolt, be burnt to nothing, but if, on the charred ground, he should come back to life again, nothing fresh would arise, only the same as before.

When you were working on him, perhaps you yourself felt unconsciously the objective greatness of this character, for whereas you generally give your characters stinging slaps in the face, him you treat with nothing but a caustic, almost respectful irony. And there is no other way: what can you add, what slap can you give – to add to that horrific detail of the *carriage*!

Because of this, *he will never hang himself*, as you will see for yourself as you get toward the end. He might change in any way you want, that is, become ever worse, lose all he has gained, move into a peasant hovel, suffer all manner of humiliation, and perish on the dung heap like an old, cast-off galosh, but be inwardly resurrected – no, no, no! A catastrophe might bring his end, but *he* will not lay hands on himself! He might just take to the bottle – that's another possible, purely Russian way out of the noose!

I followed the course of a similar character, well known to me personally, who shut himself up in his corner. As much an acquisitor as your Judas, and an adulterer, not a casual one like your hero, but out and out and past restraint. He brought his wife to despair and cast her off, regarded his children as so many young pigs, and did nothing else but clip off parcels of land from the peasants and do the round of their wives and daughters, packing off the husbands and fathers to faraway villages that he also owned to stop them interfering. Everybody shunned him, both outsiders and his own people, but he firmly kept on living unabashed in his back-of-beyond, and once he told *me* himself . . . that his peasants and house serfs were dead set against him and might be ready enough to "get rid of him," "but," he finished by saying, "I'll show them!"

And he would have shown them, too, had they not been quick. A couple of months after my visit, two husbands he had wronged and a third man he had aggrieved by cutting off a piece of his land lay in wait for him as he took a walk one evening and literally gutted him, that is, slit open his belly and spilt his innards.

That's the kind of Sedan possible for such characters.

After all, to stick a knife in yourself, to put a bullet in your head, means that you are conscious of the horror of your situation, of the bleak prospect of your downfall, it means that you feel some inner self – no, in such a character the strength for this is lacking, the material just is not there! Only a chicken-hearted fear might drive him to make the attempt (as happens with the weak-nerved), but even for this you need plenty of imagination – and that can only drive *him* into some dark corner to hide his head.

That is how I see his nature! I shall look forward to its appearance in book form: that alone, I think, will enable the reader to distinguish it from the mass of your other works that are purely subjective and devoted to the fleeting issues of the day.

Extracts from the Journal Text

[Saltykov provided two footnotes to the journal text, the first stating why it was written, the second explaining the repetition of the section recounting Porfirii's interview with Ulita that had already appeared in "Escheated."]

(i) I ask the readers to forgive me for returning to an episode that I have already touched on. [In "Escheated" the birth of Evpraksiia's baby was recounted in a dozen lines; the interview in which Porfirii arranges his dispatch with Ulita to the foundlings' home was, though, presented fully as in the final text. – ED.] After the publication of "Escheated" (*NF*, no. 8 [1876]) I had occasion several times to hear that I had not sufficiently developed the relations of Judas toward his new bastard family in the shape of the second Volodka. And since these relations represent, in the life of Judas, a characteristic moment, I have decided to make good this omission by the present story. To those who by now are weary of the tale of Judas it is, I think, appropriate to make this announcement: one more story – and the family chronicle of the house of Golovlyov will finally be concluded. (*NF*, no. 12 [1876]: 483; *SS*, 13: 688)

(ii) This scene has already appeared in the story "Escheated," but it is, by force of circumstances, essential here. In the separate edition of *The Golovlyov Chronicle* appropriate changes will be made. (*NF*, no. 12 [1876]: 508; *SS*, 13:688)

PASSAGE DELETED FROM "[ILLICIT] FAMILY JOYS"

[The deletions made in preparing the journal text for separate publication, when not demanded by the requirements of consistency, mostly served the purpose of avoiding excessive length. The following passage, which occurred in the description of Porfirii's state of mind when faced with the prospect of being revealed as a fornicator (*SS*, 13:185) may have been cut in the interests of economy, but the last two short paragraphs contain material Saltykov may have thought inappropriate at this stage of his narrative. First, there are Porfirii's thoughts of a sudden, violent release from his predicament (the imagined railway and coach accidents), which could be seen as foreshadowing his thoughts of suicide in "The Reckoning" – though, equally, he might be thinking of the chance elimination of Evpraksiia(!) – and then there is the summary statement concerning the "strange psychological process" that was taking place in him. Both these matters received due treatment in the final stages of the novel, and it may well be that Saltykov considered that reference to them here was premature.]

Even his devotions, previously so exact and clear, had, with the oncoming "disaster," become much confused. It was not so much praying, as rather a desperate effort to kill off the "disaster" by the words of his prayer. And since "mental" praying gave him but little help, he began speaking the words aloud, as if by crying [them] out he hoped to distract his mind from the abominable prospect of the "disaster." But the "disaster" defeated even these ploys in praying. Everywhere, at all times, it confronted him; it confused his tongue and made him utter totally unfitting words (for instance, concerning "a happy delivery"), which, being linked with the idea of adultery (Pshaw! Pshaw!), had so far never entered into the scheme of his usual prayers. It turned out that it was not the prayer that killed off the "disaster," but the other way round. And while his lips went on muttering words deprived of any inner meaning, so, in turn, his mind, in thrall to disordered, conflicting thoughts, itself divided in two. One moment there is the thought of "a happy delivery," then from some distant recess comes the conjecture: What if there was none of all this? What if suddenly . . . ? The latter thought nags him with particular persistence. A faint presence at first, but then it grows

– and grows until it shifts from the realm of supposition into the realm of actual realization. Judas stands before the icon with his palms together, but his lips no longer move and his eyes are not uplifted, but stare apathetically through the window at the endless expanse of the realm of winter.

His fleeting thoughts oppress him. From somewhere a railway appears: a carriage . . . the tender . . . a rock on the track . . . Crash! – and nothing! Then a *troika*: a sledge . . . the rutted track . . . unschooled horses . . . Crash! – again nothing! And finally, some simple piece of magic – and nothing, all over and done with!

In short, there was taking place in Judas some strange, unceasing psychological process. The official thoughts that he forced into his mind were striving to kill the elemental thoughts that arose naturally within him.

Extract from "Haven Home"

[Some time after publishing "Escheated" in August 1876 Saltykov attempted to write a final chapter entitled "Haven Home" to round off the Golovlyov chronicle. This attempt was abandoned and the novel was concluded with "The Reckoning" only in 1880. Unlike the profoundly serious conclusion provided by "The Reckoning," "Haven Home" was a lighthearted venture that was to show Porfirii falling victim to a plot hatched by Nadezhda Ivanovna Galkina (his cousin, the mistress of Goriushkino) to marry him off to one of her daughters and thus secure the Golovlyovo estate. "The Reckoning," in fact, ends with a reference to Galkina, who has been keeping a watch on affairs at Golovlyovo in order to take over the property on the extinction of the last Golovlyovs. The following extract from the fragment (*SS*, 13: 610–12) describes the visit of Galkina's son to Porfirii Golovlyov (to whom he presents a bottle of *rakia* – plum brandy) for the purpose of interesting him in his sister. We see Porfirii maintaining his familiar banal prattle and, given still to senile concupiscence, taking the bait offered by young Galkin in the shape of his sister Nisochka. Few would dispute that Saltykov was right to abandon this comic end to Porfirii in favor of the somber conclusion eventually provided by "The Reckoning."

The fragment was first published in 1914 by V. P. Kranikhfel'd: "Novaia ekskursiia v Golovlëvo (K 25-letnei godovshchine smerti M. E. Saltykova)," *Russkoe bogatstvo*, no. 4 (1914). In fact Saltykov used a part of "Haven Home" in "The Reckoning": the description of the winter landscape and approaching sledge with which "The Reckoning" opens is a slightly amended version of the passage describing Ganechka Galkin's arrival at Golovlyovo in "Haven Home."]

Judas was momentarily sorrowful and placed the palms of his hands together as a sign of devotional serenity, but then suddenly went on:

"Previously Goriushkino belonged to us, the Golovlyovs, but then Aunt Varvara Mikhailovna, God rest her soul . . . Still, why rake all that up! There's no use crying over spilt milk – am I right?"

Ganechka made no reply, only cast his eyes down slightly as though he understood himself to be at fault.

"So my dear cousin is in fine fettle?" Porfirii Vladimirych continued. "Well, God grant she may be. As concerns me, you can see, young nephew, for yourself. I'm getting old, my boy. I can still clump about the house and can get myself to church, too, but as for outings and visitors – that's all in the past now for me. Anyway, what business do we old men have to go thinking about amusements! We have to think, dear boy, of what answer we shall give *there*!"

Judas stood up and, looking up at the icon, whispered [something] with his lips.

Ganechka followed suit; he stood up and crossed himself.

"When I was a young man, I was fond of amusements, too. Dancing, going to the theater, eating dainties, and 'Out in the garden, in the vegetable patch . . . ' – however that song of yours goes – yes, I did all that! But now, especially since dear Mother passed away, I've given it all up. I live like a monk and pray to God. I say a prayer, sit for a while, have a bite to eat – a drop of soup, a bit of roast . . . and then again . . . That, my boy, is the life I lead!"

"Tss . . . ," muttered Ganechka, not knowing how to express his respect.

"So, you've been fighting the Turks? [i.e., as one of the Russian volunteers who supported Serbia and Montenegro in the war of 1876 – ED.] Yes, I heard about that, my boy, I did hear of it! Anpetov, one of our local gentry, went off there, too. There's a Russian Garibaldi [the Russian commander, General Cherniaev – ED.] they say has appeared, he sent off for the singers from Chudov monastery. As I see it, though, the Turks are no different . . . are the Turks not a people as much as anyone else? Only they don't eat pork, but that's no business of ours!"

"The Serbs, though, Uncle, practically live on pork."

"There you are! Everyone has his own ways: one likes melon, another likes pig's gristle. Christ be with them!"

"Quite right, Uncle."

"And you can't pass judgment on anybody for that, besides which it's a sin to pass judgment, and that's why I never do."

"Tss . . . ," said Ganechka again.

"I don't eat pork myself, and why should anyone declare war on me for that! Still, I'm not referring to you, my boy. You did your job, went and fought, and you brought me this bottle here of – what do you call it? – *raki-kaki*. . . . We shall try it at dinner; let's just see what this *kaki* is that the Serbs make."

Judas gave Ganechka a friendly pat on the knee, at which Ganechka, instead of answering, leaped up and kissed his uncle's shoulder.

"There, there, thank you, thank you! I treat you as kith and kin, my boy, the Golovlyov way. One thing, though, before I forget. I think you have sisters, haven't you?"

"Yes, Uncle, six of them."

"Well, indeed God has blessed my cousin, she has someone to gladden her heart. I had two sons myself, and I loved them, and was joyful, and had high hopes. . . . But God took them and turned my hopes to naught. And what age would my oldest niece be?"

"She's coming twenty, Uncle."

"Coming twenty, eh? In her prime then and time to be married. And her name?"

"Nisochka, Uncle."

"Anis'ia, that is . . . Just a minute, just a minute! Anisia the Roman has her feast day on . . . no, that's wrong, it's Melania the Roman who is celebrated on the thirty-first of December, and Anisia is only a martyr and is celebrated the day before."

"Exactly right, Uncle."

In such talk the time was passed until dinner. At dinner Judas was even more loquacious; he tried the *rakia* and praised it. Then he took up the subject of religion, saying that there are different faiths, but only one God for all, and that often a single idle word gives rise to religious disputes and schisms, and that all this is caused by human pride. From pride, men took it into their heads to build the Tower of Babel, but God went and confounded them. And after that when they talked they did not understand one another. And that is why there are foreign languages. Before, they all had the same language, but now without foreign languages you cannot even enter government service.

For his part, Ganechka told various things about Serbia – that the Serbs had a prince called Milan and he had a wife called Nataliia who was a Russian, while the Montenegrins had a prince called Nikolai and he had a wife called Milena; that all these were mentioned in the prayers in churches and were referred to as of the true faith; that the Moldavians had a prince and a princess, and that in the churches there, instead of "*Gospodi, pomilui*," they sing "Domine, mirveshti" [i.e., "Lord, have mercy," the first in Church Slavonic, the second in – garbled – Rumanian ("Doamne, milueşte")]; that the Turks were afraid of the Montenegrins because they cut off people's ears and noses, but they were not afraid of the Serbs, because the Serbs are a peaceful people who just make *rakia* and graze pigs.

In a word, both uncle and nephew were well contented with each other, so that when Ganechka left to go home, Porfirii Vladimirych not only invited him personally to visit Golovlyovo but told him to convey to his dearest cousin that he was expecting her to come as well . . . with Nisochka.

All in all, the young Galkin's visit had such an enlivening effect on Judas that, after his nephew's departure, he did not go directly to his study but called first to see Evpraksiia and, in token of letting bygones be bygones, gently stroked her on the back . . .

IV   SELECT BIBLIOGRAPHY

Select Bibliography

TEXT OF "THE GOLOVLYOVS"

There are numerous Russian editions of *The Golovlyovs*, published separately or in collections of Saltykov's works. The standard text is that of
the second edition of 1883. The best edited version is in Saltykov's
Sobranie sochinenii v dvadtsati tomakh (Moscow: Khudozhestvennaia literatura, 1965–77), vol. 13, which includes an extensive commentary, details of textual history, and variants from the journal text.

BIBLIOGRAPHIES OF WORKS ON SALTYKOV

L. M. Dobrovol'skii, *Bibliografiia literatury o M. E. Saltykove-
Shchedrine, 1848–1917* (Moscow-Leningrad: Akademiia nauk,
1961).
V. N. Baskakov, *Bibliografiia literatury o Saltykove-Shchedrine, 1918–
1965* (Moscow-Leningrad: Nauka, 1966).
V. N. Baskakov, "Bibliografiia literatury o Saltykove-Shchedrine,
1965–1974," in *Saltykov-Shchedrin 1826–1976. Stat'i, materialy,
bibliografiia* (Leningrad: Nauka, 1976), 391–428.
[These bibliographies list 214 items devoted to *The Golovlyovs*]
I. P. Foote, "M. E. Saltykov-Shchedrin in English: a Bibliography,"
Oxford Slavonic Papers, New Series 22 (1989): 89–114.

BIOGRAPHY

S. A. Makashin, [1] *Saltykov-Shchedrin, Biografiia 1*, (Moscow:
Gosudarstvennoe izdatel'stvo khudozhestvennoi literatury, 1949; 2d
ed., 1951); [2] *Saltykov-Shchedrin. Na rubezhe 1850–1860 godov*
(Moscow: Khudozhestvennaia literatura, 1972); [3] *Saltykov-
Shchedrin. Seredina puti, 1860-e—1870-e gody* (Moscow:
Khudozhestvennaia literatura, 1984); [4] *Saltykov-Shchedrin.
Poslednie gody, 1875–1889* (Moscow: Khudozhestvannaia literatura,
1989).
A comprehensive, originally researched biography by the
foremost Saltykov scholar. Material relevant to *The Golovlyovs* is in

volume 1, pages 11–79 (on Saltykov's early life and family background) and in volume 4, pages 215–25 (discussion of the novel).

L. Turkov, *Saltykov-Shchedrin*, 2d ed. (Moscow: Molodaia gvardiia, 1965).

A readable popular biography in the series *Lives of Remarkable People*.

CRITICAL WORKS ON SALTYKOV AND "THE GOLOVLYOVS"

In Russian

Collections of articles, reviews, etc.

N. Denisiuk, ed., *Kriticheskaia literatura o proizvedeniiakh M. E. Saltykova-Shchedrina*, 5 vols. (Moscow: Izdanie A. S. Panafidinoi, 1905).

Excerpts from reviews, articles, and critical studies written up to 1899. Items relating to *The Golovlyovs* appear in volumes 3–5.

N. M. Pokrovskii, ed., *M. E. Saltykov-Shchedrin kak satirik, khudozhnik i publitsist. Iz kriticheskoi literatury o Saltykove* (Moscow, 1906).

A single-volume compilation on the same lines as Denisiuk's.

M. S. Goriachkina, ed., *M. E. Saltykov-Shchedrin v russkoi kritike* (Moscow: Gosudarstvennoe izdatel'stvo khudozhestvennoi literatury, 1959).

Articles on Saltykov, together with letters and comments about him by notable Russian writers.

Individual Studies on Saltykov and "The Golovlyovs"

A. S. Bushmin, *Satira Saltykova-Shchedrina* (Moscow-Leningrad: Akademiia nauk, 1959). For *The Golovlyovs*, see pages 171–94.

A major study that traces the continuity and evolution of Saltykov's outlook in his satires (part 1) and examines his "artistic principles" (part 2). Strongly "social" view of *The Golovlyovs*, the chapter devoted to it concerned mostly with Porfirii as representative of the gentry class.

A. I. Efimov, *Iazyk satiry Saltykova-Shchedrina* (Moscow: Moskovskii universitet, 1953). See page 35 in this volume.

Ia. El'sberg, *Saltykov-Shchedrin, zhizn' i tvorchestvo* (Moscow:

Khudozhestvennaia literatura, 1953). For *The Golovlyovs*, see pages 391–412.

A cursory account of the novel, mainly concerned with its social-economic (class) aspect.

Ia. El'sberg, *Stil' Shchedrina* (Moscow: Khudozhestvennaia literatura, 1940). See page 35 in this volume.

M. S. Goriachkina, *Satira Saltykova-Shchedrina* (Moscow: Prosveshchenie, 1965). For *The Golovlyovs*, see pages 97–140.

Classically Soviet in its social interpretation; some useful discussion of the novel's connections with other works by Saltykov, also of landscape and language.

K. N. Grigor'ian, *Roman M. E. Saltykova-Shchedrina "Gospoda Golovlëvy"* (Moscow-Leningrad: Akademiia nauk, 1962).

Though limited in scope, a valuable study. Three chapters treat, respectively, the psychology of Porfirii, comparisons and portraiture, and landscape. The latter two chapters discuss the treatment of these features in the novel and in Saltykov's earlier work and indicate their "psychological" function in *The Golovlyovs*. The chapter on Porfirii ("Psikhologizm") is particularly recommended.

V. Kirpotin, *Mikhail Evgrafovich Saltykov-Shchedrin, zhizn' i tvorchestvo* (Moscow: Sovetskii pisatel', 1955). For *The Golovlyovs*, see pages 355–71.

This is the third, enlarged edition of a work first published in 1939. Discussion of *The Golovlyovs* mainly refers to the social theme and insists that the psychology of Porfirii is social (not individual). There is a section on Saltykov's literary views and practice (568–682).

D. Nikolaev, *M. E. Saltykov-Shchedrin, zhizn' i tvorchestvo. Ocherk.* (Moscow: Detskaia literatura, 1985). For *The Golovlyovs*, see pages 151–85.

An objective study written for younger readers. Concentrates on Golovlyovo and its significance, the psychological portrayal of Porfirii, and the "tragicomic" element in the novel. Contains interesting original observations.

E. Pokusaev, *Revoliutsionnaia satira Saltykova-Shchedrina* (Moscow: Gosudarstvennoe izdatel'stvo khudozhestvennoi literatury, 1963). For *The Golovlyovs*, see pages 385–437. See the following item.

E. Pokusaev, *"Gospoda Golovlëvy" M. E. Saltykova-Shchedrina* (Moscow: Khudozhestvennaia literatura, 1975).

An expanded version of the chapter on *The Golovlyovs* in Pokusaev's *Revoliutsionnaia satira*. Discusses Saltykov's views on the aims of the contemporary novel, then examines in detail the thematic aspects of *The Golovlyovs*, claiming its social interest as an attack on the gentry class, of which Porfirii is the essential embodiment. There is detailed analysis of Porfirii, the major Golovlyov characters, and other social elements represented in the novel. Style and language are not considered.

V. V. Prozorov, *Saltykov-Shchedrin. Kniga dlia uchitelia* (Moscow: Prosveshchenie, 1988). For *The Golovlyovs*, see pages 107–34.

A helpful, temperately written account in a Teacher's Guide to Saltykov. Deals sensibly with the novel's origins and composition, the characters, and the nature and fate of Porfirii. An extract appears in section 2 of this volume.

In English

M. Ehre, "A Classic of Russian Realism: Form and Meaning in *The Golovlyovs*," *Studies in the Novel* (Denton, Texas), 9 (1977): 3–16 (printed in section 2 of this volume).

I. P. Foote, "M. E. Saltykov-Shchedrin: *The Golovlyov Family*," *Forum for Modern Language Studies* (St Andrews) 4, no. 1 (1968): 53–63.

A general article; part of it (on style) is printed in section 2 of this volume.

H. Gifford, *The Novel in Russia, from Pushkin to Pasternak* (London: Hutchinson University Library, 1964).

A chapter on *The Golovlyovs* (97–108) succinctly makes a number of important points.

K. D. Kramer, "Satiric Form in Saltykov's *Gospoda Golovlevy*," *The Slavic and East European Journal* 14, no. 4 (1970): 453–64 (printed in section 2 of this volume).

V. S. Pritchett, *The Living Novel* (London: Chatto and Windus, 1946). Includes a chapter on *The Golovlyovs* ("The Hypocrite"), printed in section 2 of this volume.

N. Strelsky, *Saltykov and the Russian Squire* (New York: Columbia University Press, 1940; reprint: New York: AMC Press, 1966).

A study of Saltykov's presentation of the landed gentry in his works. Three central chapters examine his portrayal of the class in his "running-commentary" social sketches of the 1850s to 1860s; *The Golovlyovs*, in which there is a shift of focus from the mundane to the spiritual/moral condition of the gentry; and *Old Times in*

Poshekhon'e, Saltykov's broad portrayal of the gentry way of life before the emancipation, which had a lasting effect on the Russian social mentality. An extract from the chapter on *The Golovlyovs* is printed in section 2 of this volume.

W. M. Todd, "The Anti-hero with a Thousand Faces: Saltykov-Shchedrin's Porfiry Golovlev," *Studies in the Literary Imagination* (Atlanta, Ga.) 9, no. 1 (1976): 87–105.

An individual reading of *The Golovlyovs* that sees Porfirii as a parody of the traditional "hero" figure (portents at birth, journeys of quest, etc.) and finds in the novel parody of Rousseau, Aksakov, and Dostoevsky.

In French

K. Sanine, *Saltykov-Chtchédrine, sa vie et ses oeuvres* (Bibliothèque russe de l'Institut d'études slaves, 29) (Paris: Institut d'études slaves de l'Université de Paris, 1955).

The only full-scale book on Saltykov in a Western language. The chapter on *The Golovlyovs* (212–23) gives a well-considered account of the Saltykov-Golovlyov family links and of the fate of the main Golovlyov characters.

ENGLISH TRANSLATIONS OF "THE GOLOVLYOVS"

The Gollovlev Family, trans. Athelstan Ridgway (London: Jarrold and Sons, [1916]).

A Family of Noblemen, trans. A. Yarmolinsky (New York: Boni and Liveright, 1917).

The Golovlyov Family, trans. Natalie Duddington, introduction by Edward Garnett (London: Allen and Unwin, 1931); published also in New York (Macmillan, 1931); and reprinted in 1934 (London: Dent; New York: Dutton; this edition [in Everyman's Library] reissued in 1968 and 1974), 1968 (London: Heron), and 1977 (Westport, Conn.: Hyperion).

Judas Golovlyov, ed. Olga Shartse (Moscow: Foreign Languages Publishing House, [1957]). This is the Duddington translation slightly amended. Reissued in 1975 as *The Golovlyovs*, with an introduction by S. A. Makashin (Moscow: Progress).

The Golovlovs, trans. Andrew R. MacAndrew, afterword by William E. Harkins (New York: The New American Library, 1961).

The Golovlyov Family, trans. Samuel D. Cioran, introduction by Carl
  D. Proffer (Ann Arbor, Mich.: Ardis, 1977).
The Golovlevs, trans. and with an introduction and notes by I. P. Foote
  (Oxford: Oxford University Press, 1986).
The Golovlyov Family, trans. and with an introduction by Ronald
  Wilks. Introductory essay ("The Hypocrite") by V. S. Pritchett
  (Harmondsworth: Penguin, 1988).

ENGLISH TRANSLATIONS OF OTHER MAJOR WORKS BY
SALTYKOV

Fables. trans. Vera Volkhovsky (London: Chatto and Windus, 1931). A
  selection of Saltykov's *Fables* (*Skazki*).
Tales from M. Saltykov-Shchedrin, trans. Dorian Rottenberg (Moscow:
  Foreign Languages Publishing House, [1956?]). Another selection
  of *Fables*.
The History of a Town, trans. and with an introduction and notes by
  I. P. Foote (Oxford: Willem A. Meeuws, 1980); ibid., trans. and ed.
  Susan C. Brownsberger (Ann Arbor, Mich.: Ardis, 1982).
The Pompadours: A Satire on the Art of Government, trans. and with an
  introduction by David Magarshak (Ann Arbor, Mich.: Ardis, 1985).
  A translation of *Pompadury i pompadurshi* (Pompadours and
  pompadouresses).